The Spanish Army in North America 1700–1793

René Chartrand • Illustrated by David Rickman

Series editor Martin Windrow

First published in Great Britain in 2011 by Osprey Publishing,
Midland House, West Way, Botley, Oxford, OX2 0PH, UK
44-02 23rd Street, Suite 219, Long Island City, NY 11101, USA
E-mail: info@ospreypublishing.com

OSPREY PUBLISHING IS PART OF THE OSPREY GROUP

A CIP catalog record for this book is available from the British Library

Print ISBN: 978 1 84908 597 7
PDF ebook ISBN: 978 1 84908 598 4
ePub ebook ISBN: 978 1 84908 902 9

Editor: Martin Windrow
Page layout by Melissa Orrom Swan, Oxford
Index by Marie-Pierre Evans
Typeset in Helvetica Neue and ITC New Baskerville
Maps by The Map Studio
Originated by United Graphics Pte
Printed in China through Worldprint Ltd.

11 12 13 14 15 10 9 8 7 6 5 4 3 2 1

Osprey Publishing is supporting the Woodland Trust, the UK's leading
woodland conservation charity, by funding the dedication of trees.

www.ospreypublishing.com

Dedication

To the memory of the late Detmar Finke, US Army historian, friend,
and pioneer of Hispanic-American military material culture studies

Author's Note

This small volume attempts to present a sizable part of the military
organization and material culture of a vast portion of the truly enormous
Spanish overseas empire during nearly all of the 18th century. (For the
purposes of this study, North America includes the southern Caribbean coastal
colonies before the 1750s.) In many cases only a brief outline can be given,
but the basic sources are cited to guide further studies of these varied topics;
and despite the inevitable limitations of space, the text does quote from many
archive documents never before published, which allow the reconstruction
here for the first time of a number of uniforms.

We have used Spanish names and titles in most cases, excepting locations
such as e.g. Havana and St Augustine, where the English form is more familiar
to Anglophone readers. Inevitably this has led to some trifling inconsistencies,
e.g. Louisiana/Luisiana when mentioning both the place and the Spanish
regiment. As regards the uniform colors, "blue" generally denoted dark blue –
a hue which got darker during the 18th century; and in Spanish uniform terms,
"scarlet" could denote several shades of red. As usual, "gold" and "silver"
mean yellow or white metal or fabric, depending on the rank of the wearer.

Sources cited in the text

References in brackets refer to the following archival sources for manuscript
documents:

In Spain: (AGI) Archivo General de Indias, series Cuba, Santo Domingo,
Guadalajara, Panama; (AGS) Archivo General de Simancas, series Guerra
Moderna, Hacienda, Tesoro; (MN) Museo Naval

In Mexico: (AGN) Archivo General de la Nacion, series Bandos, Guerra
Indeferente, Historia [for Tropa Veterana], Reales Cedulas, Virreyes

In the United States: (ASKB) Anne S.K. Brown Military Collection, Brown
University Library; (BLCA) Bancroft Library, California Archives; (UFSC)
University of Florida, Stetson Collection

Acknowledgments

The material in this book is the result of several decades of research, during
which fellow historians, friends and institutions have always been most helpful:
Julio Albi, Giancarlo Boeri, Sydney Brinckerhoff, José M. Bueno, Detmar Finke,
Albert W. Haarmann, Joseph Hefter, Robin Inglis, John Langellier, John Powell;
the Anne S.K. Brown Military Collection at Brown University Library in
Providence, Rhode Island; the Archivo General de Indias in Sevilla, the Archivo
General de Simancas in Simancas, and the Museo Naval in Madrid, Spain; the
Archivo General de la Nacion in Mexico City; the Los Angeles County Museum
of Natural History, the New Mexico History Museum in Santa Fe, the University
of Florida in Gainesville, the Louisiana State Museum, and the Tulane
University Library in New Orleans.

Artist's Note

Readers may care to note that the original paintings from which the color
plates in this book were prepared are available for private sale. All reproduction
copyright whatsoever is retained by the Publishers. All enquiries should be
addressed to:

David Rickman, 1000 North Monroe Street, Wilmington, Delaware 19801, USA

The Publishers regret that they can enter into no correspondence upon this
matter.

THE SPANISH ARMY IN NORTH AMERICA 1700–1793

INTRODUCTION

Bernardo de Galvez (1746–86), Governor of Louisiana. This outstanding young general swept the British from the Gulf coast between 1779 and 1781, but died prematurely in Mexico City aged only 40. He is shown here wearing a general's uniform: blue coat, scarlet cuffs and waistcoat, with gold embroidery edging the coat and waistcoat. The cuffs have two rows of embroidery, indicating the rank of lieutenant-general to which he was promoted in 1783, as well as being appointed Viceroy of New Spain. (Museo Naval, Madrid)

By 1700, more than 200 years after the story of the vast Spanish overseas empire began with Columbus making landfall in what is now the Bahamas archipelago, a string of lost wars in Europe had brought Spain to its knees, both economically and diplomatically. This situation was then aggravated by a dynastic crisis, as two contenders claimed the throne: Prince Charles of Austria, and Philippe, Duke of Anjou and grandson of France's King Louis XIV. The War of the Spanish Succession that ensued in 1702 did not end until 1713–14, by which time the rivals were exhausted. France had lost some of its prestige as a world power to Britain, but it had secured the confirmation of Philippe as Felipe V, King of Spain and "the Indies."

However, Spain was not to become a French puppet state, as was quickly demonstrated by the rather ludicrous and half-hearted war that it waged in 1718–20 against France, Britain and several other countries. Thereafter, Spain's government had to confront the most pressing issue: the need to halt the nation's decline, and to restore its prestige as a viable power. In the years that followed the armed forces were thoroughly modernized, soon coming to employ standardized French-style tactics, maneuvers, weapons and uniforms. As the years passed, much of Spain's infrastructure, its cultural institutions and its government organization adopted French models, and these reforms proved very beneficial. The reign of Carlos III (1759–88) was the period of "La Illustracion" – the Enlightenment – during which time Spain was again a major power.

From 1702, all of Spain's overseas territories rallied to Felipe V as king, and they would expand greatly in North America during the 18th century. New outposts appeared in Texas and Arizona, and a massive addition of territory occurred after 1763 with the transfer of Louisiana from France to Spain. Simultaneously, "Upper" California was planted with missions and forts to counter any Russian adventures; by 1790, Spanish coastal explorations had

3

reached as far north as Alaska, and the fort of Nootka had been built on present-day Vancouver Island in British Columbia, Canada. In defense terms, the result of this expansion was a gradual shift of new responsibilities from the Caribbean Sea basin north of the Equator to the North American mainland. Up to the 1760s, the Spanish fought their European enemies largely in the Caribbean, but during the American War of Independence (1779–83) battles were fought mostly in Louisiana and Florida. By then, the Spanish metropolitan army numbered some 89,000 men and the regular colonial troops overseas about 15,000 men. Disciplined militiamen in North America may have amounted to about another 25,000, most of them in New Spain (Mexico). The strategic aims decided by King Carlos III had been to drive the British out of Florida, the Gulf of Mexico and the east bank of the Mississippi in North America, and, in Europe, to retake Gibraltar and Minorca. Except for stubborn Gibraltar, all these objectives were successfully achieved by 1783.

CHRONOLOGY

(Spanish units known to have participated in the various actions are indicated in brackets; artillery and staff were also present in most engagements.)

1702 War of the Spanish Succession. British repulsed at St Augustine, Florida. (Florida companies)

1713 End of War of the Spanish Succession

1718–20 War with France. Pensacola taken by French, retaken by Spanish, taken again by French in 1719, and finally returned to Spain by treaty. (Florida companies)

1739 War of Jenkins' Ear against Britain. British capture Portobello. (Detachment Panama Battalion)

1740, June British again repulsed at St Augustine. (Florida companies)

1741, March–May British repulsed at Cartagena de Indias. (Regts Cartagena, Espana, Aragon, Toledo, Lisboa, Navarra, det. marines, city militia)

1742

July Spanish repulsed at Frederica, Georgia. (Florida companies)

September British once again repulsed at St Augustine. (Florida companies)

1743, April British repulsed at St Augustine yet again. (Florida companies)

1759 War declared between Spain and Great Britain – Seven Years' War

1762, 23 August Havana falls to British. (Regts Havana, Aragon, Espana, Toledo, Edimburgo Dragoons, det. marines, city militia)

1763

19 February Treaty of Paris ends the war; Spain loses Florida, but gains Louisiana west of Mississippi.

1769, July–August Spanish take formal possession of Louisiana. (Regts Havana, Lisboa, dets. Aragon and Guadalajara, dets. America Dragoons, Havana Militia)

Foundation of San Diego, California; other *presidios* and missions established in California during the years that follow.

1779

8 May War declared between Spain and Great Britain

7 September Spanish capture Fort Bute at Manchac from British

22–23 September Spanish take Baton Rouge and Natchez from British. (dets. Regt Luisiana & Louisiana Militia, and New Orleans Distinguished Carabiniers)

28 November Fort Omoa, Honduras, taken by British, is recaptured. (Dets. Guatemala, Guatemala Dragoons, militias)

1780

9–14 March Spanish capture Mobile. (Regt Espana, dets. Luisiana, Havana, Principe, Louisiana Militia, and New Orleans Distinguished Carabiniers)

26 April British take Fort San Juan, Nicaragua. (Det. Regt Guatemala)

26 May Spanish repulse British and Indian attack on St Louis – now Missouri, but then in Louisiana. (Det. Regt Luisiana, St Louis Militia)

August Spanish retake Fort San Juan. (Dets. Regt Castilla de Campeche, Guatemala Dragoons, militias)

1781

2 January Spanish capture Fort St Joseph, Illinois, from British. (Det. Louisiana Militia)

7 January British attack on Las Aldeas near Mobile repulsed. (Dets. Regts Havana, Principe, Espana, Navarra, and Louisiana Militia)

10 March–9 May Spanish siege and capture of British Pensacola. (Regts Soria, Corona, Aragon, Rey, Guadalajara, Hibernia, Flandes, Napoles, 2nd Catalonian Volunteers, Espana, Navarra, Zamora, Extremadura, Leon, Principe; dets. Toledo, Mallorca, Luisiana, Havana; Luisiana Dragoons, America Dragoons, det. Louisiana Militia, Havana grenadiers of Mulatto and Morenos Militia)

28 June Spanish recapture Natchez, taken by British in May. (Dets. Regt Luisiana, Louisiana Militia)

1782

March Roatan Island, Honduras, and posts on the coast taken by Spanish. (Regts Navarra, Guatemala, det. Castilla de Campeche, Guatemala Dragoons, militias)

12 April Franco-Spanish fleet defeated by British in naval battle of The Saints. (Aragon as marines)

8 May Spanish capture Nassau, Bahamas. (Regts Guadalajara, Espana, New Spain's Corona Regt, Havana Pardo and Moreno dets.)

30 August British retake Roatan Island. (Regts Navarra, Guatemala) Spanish expeditions against Indians of Darien Coast, on Pacific southeast of Panama (Regt Corona), and Mosquito Coast, on Carribean northeast of Fort San Juan (Regt Hibernia)

1783

18 April British retake Nassau, Bahamas.

3 September Peace treaty ends war; Spain regains East and West Florida from British.

1790

Spanish establish a post with regular garrison (Catalonian Volunteers to 1794, det. San Blas company thereafter) at Nootka on present-day Vancouver Island, Canada, and explore coast up to Alaska. After friction with Britain, Nootka evacuated in 1795.

1793

7 March Spain declares war on the French Republic.

THE OVERSEAS ARMY

Regular troops, 1700–63

In the early 16th century, Spanish soldiers overseas were adventurers, led by leaders who would seek out new domains to conquer and then to govern. Forts were built, and small numbers of soldiers were hired to guard the important port cities such as Havana in Cuba, Vera Cruz in New Spain (now Mexico), and San Juan, Puerto Rico.[1] A defense system thus evolved for the colonies north of the Equator; this featured troops stationed in powerful forts, which were all linked to one another by the movements of the treasure fleets that, ultimately, assembled in Havana before sailing for Spain. This defensive strategic outlook remained essentially unchanged until the end of the Seven Years' War in 1763. On the American mainland, the northern frontier of New Spain was protected from hostile Indians by a string of fortified posts called *presidios*; often co-located with religious missions, these were established and garrisoned by mounted soldiers nicknamed the "Cuera dragoons."

Until the early 18th century the regular troops guarding Spain's empire in the West were few in number, and were organized in independent companies. The Viceroy of New Spain, residing in Mexico City, was the supreme authority and commander in North America. He had a ceremonial guard of halberdiers that dated back to 1568; his palace also had a company of guard infantry, and when he traveled his carriage was escorted by his company of horse guards. Amazingly, these units were the only regular troops in central New Spain until the middle of the 18th century. (The viceroy's horse and foot guard companies were disbanded in 1765, but the halberdiers survived until 1821.)

The viceroy's subordinate in the West Indies was the Captain-General of Cuba, who had subordinate governors of Puerto Rico, Santo Domingo and Florida. These areas each had a few regular independent companies. The Captain-General of Guatemala oversaw Central America and – in practice, if not always in name – the Yucatan Peninsula. Further south were the Spanish possessions on the Caribbean coast of New Grenada (present-day Venezuela and Colombia), and in Panama. Although nominally subject to the authority of the Viceroy of Peru, and later of New Grenada, the regular companies based at the fortress city of Cartagena de Indias and in Panama were an integral part of Spain's North American defense system during the first half of the 18th century.

The first major step in the reorganization of the colonial garrisons north of the Equator occurred in 1717 at Havana, where its independent companies were grouped into a battalion, but reforms took time to reach other American garrisons. Some ten years passed before Vera Cruz raised a corps of regular dragoons, and it was another four before that port's authorities organized in 1731 a Batallon de Marina de la Armada de Borlavento ("Battalion of Marines of the Windward Fleet"), providing detachments to serve as marines aboard the treasure fleets. In 1736, a battalion that included an artillery company was organized at Cartagena de Indias. In September 1738, a battalion of seven infantry companies, one of artillery and two of cavalry was organized in Santo Domingo, on the island of Hispaniola (now the Dominican Republic). In November

[1] See Osprey Fortress 49, *The Spanish Main 1492–1800*.

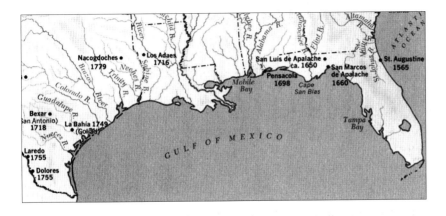

The main Spanish settlements on the Gulf of Mexico in the present-day United States. The garrisons in Texas – at Las Aldeas, and further west – consisted of the frontier *"Cuera"* cavalry guarding the Interior Provinces of northern New Spain. The garrisons in Florida were dependencies of the Captain-General of Cuba. (Map by US National Park Service)

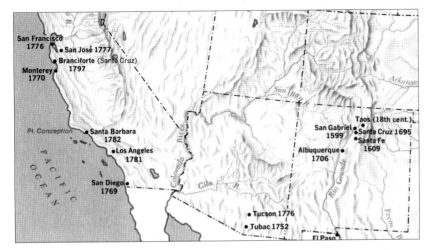

LEFT: The main Spanish settlements in the present-day American southwest and California. This huge area was dotted from Texas to northern California with *presidios* – a combination of military bases, religious missions and colonial settlements; only the main ones are shown here. (Map by US National Park Service)

BELOW: The main Spanish military bases in present-day southern Mexico, Central America, the Caribbean and northern South America.

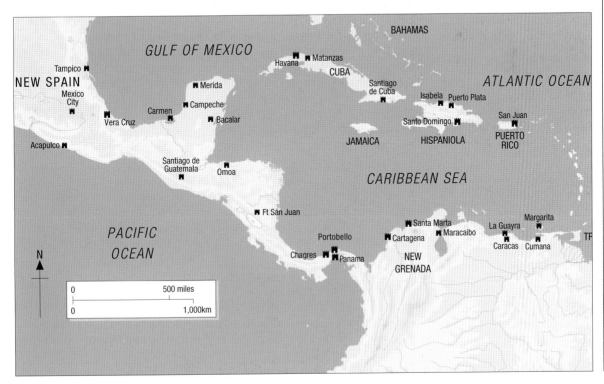

Halberdier of a viceregal guard, 1740s, from a contemporary watercolor. Each of the viceroys appointed to rule the Spanish overseas empire was provided with a ceremonial honor guard of halberdiers; the company guarding the Viceroy of New Spain was raised in 1568, and in the 1700s it consisted of two officers and 22 enlisted men. The uniform of these companies was similar to that of the King's Halberdiers in Spain: dark blue coat and breeches, scarlet cuffs, lining, waistcoat and stockings, silver buttons and lace. (Anne S.K. Brown Military Collection, Brown University Library, Providence, USA)

of the same year an infantry battalion of eight fusilier companies, one of grenadiers and one of artillery was mustered in Panama. In 1740 the Vera Cruz marine battalion was converted into a colonial battalion of five companies, serving primarily on land; retitled the Corona Regiment, it was augmented to six companies, including one of grenadiers, in 1749. At that time Vera Cruz also had a company of regular artillery, and six dragoon companies.

New Spain included the Yucatan Peninsula and Central America down to Panama; the latter was the territory of Guatemala, with the adjoining provinces of Nicaragua, Honduras, Costa Rica and El Salvador. Since the 17th century there had been a few small and isolated garrisons in those areas; in 1754, the Castilla de Campeche Battalion, consisting of five infantry companies and one of artillery, was organized to provide garrisons at Campeche, Merida and Fort Bacalar in the Yucatan. On Puerto Rico, meanwhile, the independent infantry and artillery companies had also been organized into a battalion consisting of one artillery and five infantry companies since 1739, the infantry component being reduced to four companies in 1741.

Some troops – notably those in Florida, which consisted of one artillery, one cavalry (raised since 1715) and three infantry companies – had remained independent units. On 8 April 1753, these were merged into the regular Havana Regiment; this was reorganized into a legion-like unit of four battalions, each battalion having one company of grenadiers and four of fusiliers. The regiment also had four companies of artillery and four of dragoons. Three fusilier companies, with 40 gunners and a company of dragoons, were posted at St Augustine in Florida, with men partly incorporated from the former independent companies. "Invalids" – i.e. over-age soldiers – were formed in Havana into one or two companies. Part of the regiment was present at the 1762 siege and surrender of Havana. The Florida detachments remained part of the Havana Regiment until the territory was ceded to Great Britain in 1763, and subsequently the regiment was completely reorganized.

Expansion of the overseas regular army, 1763–93

From the 1730s until the Seven Years' War, a policy of providing reinforcements detached from metropolitan army regiments in Spain had worked fairly effectively. The loss of Havana and Manila in 1762 provoked an in-depth review of the defenses guarding Spain's overseas empire. A powerful and secret committee met in Madrid; decisions were taken swiftly, and substantial funds were devoted to their implementation. Firstly, the fortifications were considerably strengthened. Secondly, the regular colonial troops were permanently reinforced with metropolitan battalions, and many new regular colonial units were raised; henceforth, colonial garrisons would routinely be composed of a mixture of both types of regular troops, rather than only being reinforced with metropolitan units at times of perceived emergency. Thirdly, the artillery in the Spanish Empire became the responsibility of the metropolitan Royal Corps of Artillery, whose new overseas establishment incorporated various colonial regular artillery units. Fourthly, the colonial militias were totally reorganized and greatly expanded – measures that were to have a profound impact on the social structure of Latin American communities.

In the age of sail Cuba and Puerto Rico were the keys to the Spanish Main. In Cuba, as soon as Havana was returned to Spain by treaty in 1763, the Havana Regiment was reorganized as an infantry regiment, with remnants of its former regular dragoon companies becoming the America Dragoons. In 1788–89, the three-battalion Cuba Regiment was organized, and its 3rd Battalion was stationed in St Augustine, Florida, from 1790 to 1815.

From 1763, Spain's possessions on the North American mainland expanded considerably. Florida had been ceded to Britain up to the east bank of the Mississippi River, but Louisiana was now under the Spanish flag. In August 1769 the remaining six French garrison companies were finally relieved at New Orleans by a strong Spanish force. Men detached from the metropolitan troops were formed into the new Fijo de Luisiana Regiment during late 1769 and 1770; headquartered in New Orleans, it sent out detachments to garrison posts mostly along the Mississippi River as far north as Illinois. Louisiana also had a regular artillery company and, from 1780, a regular dragoon company, whose role was partly constabulary.

On Puerto Rico, the inspecting Gen Alejandro O'Reilly was not very impressed by the regular Puerto Rico Regiment. It was disbanded in 1766, in favor of an experiment whereby only metropolitan units would provide the garrison's infantry. This concept was abandoned in 1790, the garrison being replaced by the usual mixed establishment of colonial and metropolitan corps, and a new regular Fijo de Puerto Rico Regiment was raised.

The regular garrison of Santo Domingo, which shared the island of Hispaniola with the French (the latter ruling present-day Haiti), was reorganized in 1771 into a 12-company infantry battalion with a regular artillery company. From that time a company of "Fieles Practicos de la Frontera" patrolled the largely mountainous border with the French colony.

In New Spain, the Corona Regiment was attached to the metropolitan America Regiment between 1765 and 1767, and was

Privates, Mexico Dragoon Regiment, c.1765, from a contemporary watercolor. Blue coat and breeches, scarlet cuffs, lapels and waistcoat, gold buttons and hat lace, brown gaiters, black boots, scarlet saddlecloth edged with yellow or gold lace, sword with white metal grip and guard. (Museo de Ejercito, Madrid)

Private's uniform of the Fijo de Luisiana Regiment, 1785: white coat, with blue collar, cuffs, turnbacks, waistcoat and breeches, silver buttons and white hat lace. Note that the artist has put the buttons on the left side in order to show them in this schematic – they were actually on the right side. Probably as a positive gesture by the Spanish government toward the inhabitants of the former French colony of Louisiana, the regiment's uniform was notably similar to that of the French colonial troops it replaced, though the French colonial Compagnies franches de la Marine had brass buttons, gold hat lace, and no coat collar. (Uniforme 54; Archivo General de Indias, Sevilla)

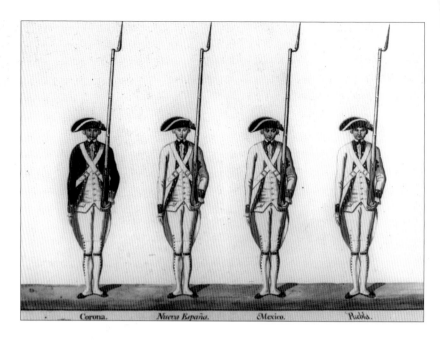

raised to two battalions. Two dragoon units, the Espana and Mexico regiments, were also raised in 1764 and 1765 respectively, incorporating the former Vera Cruz dragoon companies. A corps of 120 Invalids raised from the veterans of New Spain's regular troops served in Mexico City from about 1764; it was reorganized from 3 June 1773 into two companies, one of which was posted to Vera Cruz. In April 1767 an independent company of Catalonian Volunteers was raised in Catalonia, Spain; that August it arrived in New Spain, where it joined another company of mountain fusiliers raised in the colony at that time. In 1769 a detachment from the Catalan company took part in the California expedition that founded San Diego and Monterey. Early in 1773 the Catalonian Volunteers were reorganized as a two-company corps, incorporating the local mountain fusiliers. From 1790 to 1794 the 1st Company was stationed at the new post of Nootka on Vancouver Island, and some of its men were detached as marines on expeditions that reached Alaska. In central New Spain, the infantry regiments Nueva Espana, Mexico and Puebla were organized in 1788, and a Vera Cruz Battalion was raised in 1792.

In 1773, the Acapulco garrison company was raised to garrison that Pacific-coast port base for the "Manila galleon." From that same year, an infantry company (raised to three companies in 1780) and two companies of dragoons stood guard at the island fort of Carmen on the shores of the Gulf of Mexico. In 1780, two companies were raised to garrison the citadel of San Juan de Ulloa at Vera Cruz. The San Blas garrison company, raised from November 1788, detached 20 men to Nootka in 1794–95.

The Castilla de Campeche Battalion was expanded in 1778 to nine infantry companies including one of grenadiers, some of which were detached to campaign against the British in Central America. The Yucatan Dragoon Company was raised in 1769–70, and a garrison company was also raised for Fort Bacalar. In 1777 the Fijo de Guatemala Regiment was organized, consisting of nine companies including one of grenadiers and a company of artillery, and was augmented by a second battalion in 1782. The Fort Omoa company was raised in 1788.

The "Cuera soldiers"

From the second half of the 16th century there were cavalry soldiers posted along the northern frontier of New Spain, from the Gulf of Mexico on the Atlantic to the Gulf of California on the Pacific, yet their story is still largely unknown. The tools of their trade were shields, lances, and the leather coats that earned them their nickname: "*soldados de cuera*" ("leather soldiers"). They were a unique type of fighting force whose service involved postings dispersed over vast areas, ranging from rolling prairies to unforgiving deserts.

As the Spanish Conquistadores moved north they encountered considerable resistance from more "barbaric" (i.e. less docile) Indians, who employed skillful hit-and-run tactics. To counter these, the Spanish evolved a type of fortified village or post called a *presidio*. This center of military command for an area, usually held by a captain with a number of soldiers, was also home to their dependants, to settlers, and to Christianized Indians who gathered around a mission station. A number of these posts were built, to form an intermittent defense "line" right across northern New Spain. In time, this vast area became known as the Provincias Internas ("interior provinces") of New Spain; until 1776 these came under the direct authority of the Viceroy, but thereafter, to improve effective administration, they were set up as an independent and separate Commandancy-General.

In the 18th century most of the presidial soldiers were natives of the Interior Provinces. Many of them – about half in the 1780s – were *criollos* (white men of Spanish ancestry, born in New Spain); about a third were of mixed blood, mostly Indian and Spanish, and a minority were Indians.

The last stand of Commandant Pedro de Villasur and his "Cuera" troopers, 1720. This remarkable painting on hide, made by an Indian, depicts the fate of an expedition into the wilderness of present-day Nebraska.
It shows the cavalrymen wearing their leather coats over mostly blue and red clothing, and the wide-brimmed hat peculiar to these frontier soldiers. (Collection and photo Museum of New Mexico, Santa Fe)

The first five presidios established in the 1570s had companies of only six men each, and by the 1690s the total establishment stood at about 600 cavalrymen (more properly, dragoons). The 18th century saw considerable increases in the strength of these troops. In 1729 there were 19 companies totaling 734 men; in 1764, 23 companies with 1,271 troopers; and in 1777 the garrisons numbered 1,907 soldiers and 280 Indian scouts, which required a herd of more than 14,000 horses and 1,700 mules for their service. In 1783 the number of soldiers posted in 22 presidios was 2,840; this had increased to 3,087 in 24 presidios by 1787, and thereafter the numbers remained fairly stable. Under the regulations of 10 September 1772 a company would have 40 soldiers, but this varied greatly in practice. In 1787 there were 94 troopers in the company posted at San Antonio, Texas; 120 at Santa Fe, New Mexico; 73 at Tucson, now in Arizona; but only 33 at San Francisco, California.

Privates, Havana Blancos (white) and Morenos (colored) militia battalions, 1764. The grenadiers of both units were detached to New Orleans in 1769, and the Morenos were at the siege of Pensacola in 1781. The Havana Blancos Bn had a white uniform with black collar, cuffs, and laces on the coat front, white metal buttons and hat lace, buff accoutrements and cartridge box flap. The Havana Morenos Bn wore a red jacket with blue collar and cuffs, white metal buttons, white buttonhole lace, white breeches, black cap with a red cockade, buff accoutrements and cartridge box flap. These types of uniforms were adopted in certain other locations such as Santo Domingo, Puerto Rico and Vera Cruz. (Uniforme 26bis & 25bis, Archivo General de Indias, Sevilla)

Fighting such Indians as the Apaches and Comanches required mobility and skill in counter-guerrilla tactics. The usual pattern of warfare consisted of cavalry patrols trying to locate and engage elusive bands of Indians, while the raiders tried to slip through the network of patrols. There were a few disasters, the worst probably being the extermination of the Villasur expedition in 1720, when that imprudent Spanish commander rode far north-east of Santa Fe and was overwhelmed by Indians (possibly with the help of French-Canadian traders) in present-day Nebraska. But such a defeat had no strategic effect, and the line of frontier forts and settlements kept growing steadily. It has sometimes been concluded that the Spanish failed in their attempts to eliminate the Indian "problem," since some did slip south across the Rio Grande. The presidios were not intended to be a hermetic barrier, however, but bases for patrols, and there were more soldiers and militiamen south of this line to intercept or pursue the relatively few marauding Indians that did get through. Viewed in that light, there is no doubt that the defense of northern New Spain was a success, since the all-important objective – the safety of settled Mexico – was achieved.

Stationed far from the large centers of colonial civilization that they protected, these tough "leather soldiers" on the frontiers led a life considerably different from that of other cavalry troopers. In 1772 each of them had, by regulation, not just one but half a dozen horses, besides a colt and a mule; this gives an idea of the hard demands of their long patrols into the wilderness. Their opponents were not the polite foes of Europe's contemporary "lace wars," but ferocious warriors, and any soldier who was unfortunate enough to be taken alive might die very slowly.

For their part, an Italian traveler in 1697 noted that the frontier soldiers were "to do what they can, not to kill [the Indians], but to bring them back [to missionaries] so that they may be instructed in our Holy Religion." To what extent this ideal was honored in practice must remain a matter for conjecture. Being isolated, the soldiers had little of the formal training and discipline known in Europe – a situation deplored by Spanish Army inspecting officers, who nevertheless often admired their stamina and bravery.

These soldiers were also used to curb the territorial ambitions, real or imaginary, of other powers. The brief French appearance in Texas in 1685–87, and their settlement of Louisiana from the early 18th century, brought the Spanish there on a permanent basis. The Presidio of Las Aldeas, Texas, marked the effective border with the French at nearby Fort Natchitoches, Louisiana. Apart from the short war between France and Spain in 1718–20, relations were generally good between the fellow Bourbon monarchs on the thrones of the two countries. From 1769, California was settled and garrisoned by these frontier troops, to counter the perceived threat of a Russian descent from Alaska.

Contemporary watercolor of an officer of a rural – "provincial" – militia cavalry unit, c.1760s–70s. From his clothing and equipment, this man is probably a wealthy hacienda owner. He wears a gray hat, and a reddish poncho edged with silver lace. Beneath this can be seen a richly embroidered yellow coat with red cuffs and silver buttons, blue breeches edged with silver lace, and embroidered translucent silk stockings. The horse housings are also elaborately embroidered. This officer is armed with a broad-bladed sword, and a carbine in a saddle-holster. This general type of clothing was typical for the irregular cavalry of New Spain, although that of ordinary militiamen would be much less luxurious. (Museo de Ejercito, Madrid)

Colonial militias

Before the late 1760s the militias of Spain's overseas territories were, at best, inefficient. They were supposed to muster all able-bodied free men between the ages of 16 and 60, generally but not exclusively of Hispanic ancestry. The militiamen were grouped into companies in the towns and the countryside, and were led by officers who were usually the wealthier men of their community. Musters were rare, as were effective weapons, and uniforms were almost unheard of. For the most part, no one knew much about military maneuvers because there was no advanced training; only in a few large colonial towns such as Mexico City could one find militia companies that were well appointed and drilled, because they were made up of enthusiastic and wealthy volunteers (see illustrations). According to Nicolas Joseph de Ribera's *Descripcion* of 1760, even in Havana the urban militiamen who were supposed to muster at Easter found "a thousand excuses" not to show up, and some of the young men even considered that it was insulting to be reviewed. Some gave a good account of themselves when the British attacked Havana two years later, but the most strategically important city in the Spanish Indies nevertheless fell to the enemy. Considerable apprehension gripped other colonial port cities, and thousands of militiamen were gathered for a time at Vera Cruz to resist a rumored British attack that never occurred.

The Grenadier Company of the Silversmith's Guild, Mexico City; contemporary watercolor, c.1770. This militia unit, first organized in 1683, had about 80 members, whose wealth was indicated by a high-quality uniform: black bearskin grenadier cap with long blue bag; scarlet coat and breeches, blue cuffs, turnbacks and waistcoat, gold buttons, gold lace at the buttonholes and edging the cuffs. The belt is shown as blue, with a gilt matchcase; the musket has a buff sling, and a hanger is carried in a brown scabbard. (Museo de Ejercito, Madrid)

Colonel Juan Manuel Gonzalez de Cossio, Count Torre de Cossio, of the Toluca Provincial Infantry Regiment in New Spain, 1781. Dark blue coat, waistcoat and breeches, scarlet collar, cuffs and lining, gold buttons and garters, gold cuff and hat lace. He wears a badge of the knightly Order of Calatrava, and a cape of the Order lies on the table behind him. (Museo Nacional de Historia, Mexico City)

From 1763–64 sweeping changes were made in the organization of the colonial militia. While in Havana, Gen Alejandro O'Reilly restructured the Cuban militia, and his regulations became the basis for the organization of the militias in other colonies. Instructions coming out of Spain now called for the "disciplined" militia to be divided into "urban" city units and "provincial" corps in the countryside, drafted from men aged 16 to 45 if there were not enough volunteers. Officers were usually found amongst the educated and wealthy men of a colony, if possible those with some military experience. These units were to muster frequently, their officers and men being trained by instructors detached from the regular units; they were to be granted some fiscal and social advantages by the "Fuero Militar" system, and to be provided with basic uniforms and weapons. Some detachments of urban or provincial militia units could be called up for active duty even in peacetime; for instance, in 1769 the grenadier companies of the Havana urban militia regiments were sent to New Orleans with the regulars, to formally take possession of Louisiana from the French.

This type of organization was also introduced in other colonies, including Puerto Rico and, in 1770, for the Louisiana Militia. In 1775 a militia battalion was organized in New Orleans, followed by an artillery company in 1778, and the Distinguished Carabinier cavalry a year later. Other units followed at St Louis and St Genevieve (now in Missouri), and a "German" company was organized at Pensacola in 1784. By 1792, ten companies of "Germans and Americans" had been added in New Orleans, and many other units of infantry and cavalry elsewhere. Naturally, regulations were not always rigorously followed, especially in vast territories such as New Spain, which faced various difficulties in implementing them. Nevertheless, by 1784 the militia of New Spain had grown from perhaps a few hundred properly uniformed, armed and drilled men to over 18,000 enlisted in provincial and urban units. Another 15,000 less fully organized men were listed in companies situated mostly on the Atlantic and Pacific coastlines, and there were also hundreds of militiamen in the northern provinces, from Texas to California. The militia in Central America, officially part of New Spain, came under the immediate command of the Captain-General of Guatemala. Originally organized as companies, the militia of Guatemala was reorganized into battalions from 1779. In 1781 it was computed at 21,136 men, but only a few hundred were uniformed and well-armed "disciplined" militiamen; nevertheless, some took part in several engagements (see Chronology, and Plate H1).

THE METROPOLITAN ARMY

Until 1748 metropolitan army battalions had 13 companies – 12 of fusiliers and one of grenadiers. In that year the number of fusilier companies was reduced to eight. It was back to 13 companies from 1753 to 1760; then eight of fusiliers and one of grenadiers until 1761, when fusiliers were reduced to seven companies. From 1768 the regiment had one grenadier and nine fusilier companies, until 1791; thereafter a battalion consisted of one grenadier and four fusilier companies. Company establishment strength varied over the years. From 1768 to 1791 it was three officers and 77 NCOs and fusiliers, or 73 grenadiers. Actual company strength seemed to have hovered around 50 or 60 men in both metropolitan and colonial battalions.

Metropolitan regiments in North America, 1726–63

The first detachments of reinforcements for America from metropolitan army units appear to have been made in 1726, when a company each from the Africa and Toledo regiments were sent to the viceroyalty of New Grenada, probably to serve at Cartagena de Indias or Panama. Once in place they were simply left there, and appear to have been absorbed into the colonial troops or disbanded.

It was from the 1730s that a major policy change occurred with regards to overseas defense. Detachments of the metropolitan army would henceforth be sent as temporary reinforcements to cities in America that seemed most likely to be the targets of enemy attacks, but would eventually be brought back to Spain. The first detachments appear to have been sent out in 1733, when 200 men each from the Lisboa, Toledo and Navarra regiments sailed for Portobello and Panama. In 1737 the Murcia, Cantabria and Asturias regiments each detached two companies, and the Cataluna and Valencia regiments one company each, to reinforce the garrison of Havana (UFSC, AGI87-1-260). These eight companies, numbering more than 400 men, were stationed for some time at St Augustine, Florida, in 1739–40 (*Gentleman's Magazine*, X).

The new defense policy was tested during the conflicts with Britain between 1739 and 1748. In 1739 a half-battalion of the Navarra Regiment was sent to Portobello and Panama. Portobello and the fort of Chagres were captured by Admiral Vernon in November 1739, but Panama remained safe. Flushed with success, Vernon was back in the West Indies in 1740 leading a fleet of some 180 ships with thousands of troops on board, hoping to seize Havana, Vera Cruz and Cartagena de Indias. The Spanish

Grenadier and fusilier of an unidentified Spanish metropolitan infantry regiment, 1740s, from a contemporary watercolor. Both figures wear the standard infantry uniform, in this case white with red cuffs and waistcoats, brass buttons, false-gold hat lace, buff accoutrements and brown cartridge-box flap.
The grenadier is distinguished by his black bearskin cap with a red bag hanging from the back, and by a brass-hilted hanger. (Anne S.K. Brown Military Collection, Brown University Library, Providence, USA)

Drummer and fifer of Spanish metropolitan infantry, 1740s–50s; note that in this reconstruction the coat tails and the waistcoats are too short. From the early 18th century, regimental drummers and fifers appear to have worn the regiment's uniform trimmed with livery lace; for example, in 1751 the Milan Regiment's drummers had that regiment's white coat with blue facings, trimmed with red, white and blue lace. However, some regiments wore reversed colors; Espana's drummers are known to have had green coats in 1755 with, probably, yellow lace (because its drum major had gold lace); its drums were painted white, green and yellow, with the royal arms. Drummers and fifers of the Burgos and Guadalajara regiments had red coats with yellow lace in 1751; and in 1754, Corona's had blue coats trimmed with white and red lace. From March 1760, all drummers and fifers were to wear the colors of the royal livery – blue faced with red, and trimmed with the king's livery lace. (Print after Giminez; private collection)

ABOVE RIGHT **A private of the Fusileros de Montana, c.1745–1750. A company of this metropolitan light infantry unit was sent to Cuba in the 1740s, and transferred to St Augustine, Florida, in October 1746. This corps had a distinctive uniform incorporating some aspects of Catalonian mountaineer's costume: an amply-cut blue _gambeta_ coat with scarlet cuffs, here slung over the left shoulder; a scarlet waistcoat, blue breeches, white stockings, silver buttons, white hat lace, and buff leather sandals, accoutrements and cartridge box. He is armed with a pair of pistols, seen in a double holster on his left hip, and an _escopeta_ carbine with its bayonet. (Anne S.K. Brown Military Collection, Brown University Library, Providence, USA)**

suspected correctly that Cartagena de Indias would be Vernon's prime target, and a battalion each of the Espana and Aragon regiments were sent there in early 1740, to be joined that October by battalions of the Toledo, Lisboa and Navarra regiments. These battalions, together with the Fijo de Cartagena Battalion and 400 marines, made up 3,100 of the 4,000 defenders of that fortress city when it was besieged in March 1741, by some 12,000 British troops (including 3,600 Americans) with 15,000 Royal Navy personnel. Nevertheless, the Spanish garrison prevailed under the command of Governor Blas de Lezo, a crusty, battle-tested veteran. Repulsed in several assaults, the British and American troops were further devastated by fevers that killed thousands of men. By May 1741 some 18,000 of Vernon's soldiers and sailors were dead or sick, and he was forced to sail away. Meanwhile, a battalion of the Portugal Regiment had reached Havana in early 1740, further reinforcing that city, where it remained in garrison until 1749. Combined with the regular colonial troops already in place, these metropolitan reinforcements could make a significant difference, especially if they were posted to heavily fortified cities such as Havana, Cartagena de Indias and Vera Cruz.

Following Vernon's disastrous campaign the British realized that the Spanish were strong enough to defend their port cities, and shelved their American ambitions. In the event, both Spain's and Britain's forces became more involved in European campaigns. Few reinforcements were sent from Spain thereafter, but some do appear in the records, usually in modest numbers. In 1741 the Italica Dragoon Regiment went "to the Indies," and appears to have been disbanded in America after 1743. From 1742 to 1749 the Almanza Dragoon Regiment served in Havana (AGI, Santo Domingo 2108). In the early 1740s a company of "Fusileros de Montana" (mountain fusiliers) with 102 officers and men was sent to Havana and then, in October 1746, to St Augustine, accompanied by 36 wives and 20 children. In 1749 six officers and 135 men of the Navarra Regiment also sailed for "the Indies." In 1750, the Asturias Regiment had 70 men, and the Sevilla eight officers and 271 men, detached in America. In 1752 the

Cantabria and Murcia regiments each had six officers and 120 men in Caracas, Venezuela. In general, the troops overseas appear to have been drafted into colonial units or disbanded, although some detachments were eventually shipped home to Spain.

The Seven Years' War

In 1760, once again at war against Britain, Spain proceeded to send sizable contingents of troops to America. A battalion each of the Aragon, Espana and Toledo infantry regiments, and the Edimburgo Dragoons, were sent to Havana that year, while Murcia went to Santiago de Cuba. In 1761, two battalions of Cantabria and one battalion of Asturias reinforced Cartagena de Indias, while a battalion of Grenada first reinforced Santo Domingo, then Santiago de Cuba. The following year a battalion of Navarra further strengthened Cartagena de Indias. To reinforce Puerto Rico, a company each of Aragon and Espana were sent there in 1760, and two companies of Navarra in 1763. A company each of Toledo and Murcia joined the colonial garrison of Santo Domingo in 1760, until replaced by the 2nd Battalion of Grenada early in 1762.

Britain prevailed in this conflict, and in 1762 British forces attacked and took Havana in Cuba and Manila in the Philippines. This news raised considerable fears in other great Spanish colonial ports, and local officials mobilized and trained all the local forces they could raise. For instance, thousands of militiamen mustered and equipped themselves in the Vera Cruz area of New Spain during 1762 in anticipation of a British attack. However, by now all the participants in the Seven Years' War were exhausted, and peace was signed in early 1763.

Metropolitan regiments in North America, 1764–93

Following the end of the Seven Years' War, King Carlos III and his ministers started preparing the armed services for the next war against Britain that would inevitably break out within a few years. The army was reorganized and modernized, while the navy was rebuilt with capital ships, the size of which had never been seen before in Spain. Huge sums were expended to make Havana, San Juan (Puerto Rico) and Cartagena de Indias almost impregnable fortress cities.

Cuba, especially its capital Havana, became the main military base in North America. Besides the local regular colonial garrison, many metropolitan battalions were now posted to Havana. In April 1763 the Cordoba Regiment was shipped to Havana, where it helped to reorganize the Fijo de Habana Regiment before returning to Spain in 1765. It was replaced by the Lisboa Regiment until 1769, followed by Sevilla and Irlanda in 1770–71, by Aragon and Guadalajara from 1771 to 1774, by Principe from 1771 until 1782, by Espana in 1776, Navarra in 1779, Napoles in 1780–82, and subsequently by other units.

The transfer of Louisiana from France to Spain was a gradual process between 1766 and 1769 when, following some resistance

Ensign and private of the Aragon metropolitan infantry regiment, 1740s. A battalion of this regiment, and one of Navarra, were sent in 1740 to Cartagena de Indias in present-day Colombia, where they formed an outstanding part of the garrison that repulsed the British and Americans who besieged that fortress city from March to May 1741. White uniform with scarlet collar, cuffs and waistcoat, gold buttons and hat lace.
The regimental color shown has the regiment's coat of arms at each end of the red "ragged cross," but did not actually have the regiment's name inscribed – this has simply been added to the flags in this most valuable manuscript collection of watercolors in order to identify the units portrayed. (Detail from plate also showing Navarra; Anne S.K. Brown Military Collection, Brown University Library, Providence, USA)

17

Fusiliers of the Espana, Toledo and Mallorca metropolitan infantry regiments, from a hand-colored printed drill manual of 1762; the Espana and Toledo formed part of the Havana garrison during the siege of that year. All have white coats and breeches and yellow metal buttons, and note the large ventral cartridge box with a reddish-brown flap:
Espana – green collar and cuffs, white waistcoat.
Toledo – white collar, blue cuffs and waistcoat.
Mallorca – white collar, scarlet cuffs and waistcoat.
(Anne S.K. Brown Military Collection, Brown University Library, Providence, USA)

from the French settlers, a large force was sent to New Orleans. This included the Lisboa, Aragon and Guadalajara metropolitan infantry regiments, the Havana colonial regiment, and companies of Havana's Moreno and Pardo Militia (both these Spanish terms for "brown," "dark" or "swarthy" indicated the racial make-up of this militia).

Detachments from the garrison in Cuba were sent to Louisiana and used with great success by the young and energetic Governor Galvez in 1779 and 1780, when he conquered most of British West Florida. In March 1781, a Spanish force of about 8,000 men from metropolitan and colonial regiments undertook the siege of Pensacola. This was the largest operation by the Spanish forces during the American War of Independence, and Pensacola's British garrison surrendered on 9 May. Spanish operations in Florida ceased thereafter, as there was no strategic value to conquering British East Florida.

Spanish forces did take Nassau in the Bahamas in 1782, but most metropolitan units assembled in the French colony of Saint-Domingue (now Haiti) for a projected Franco-Spanish invasion of British Jamaica. This was never attempted, however, due to the defeat of Adm de Grasse's French fleet at the battle of The Saints by Adm Rodney's Royal Navy squadron. Nevertheless, most British islands and all of West Florida were now occupied by Spanish or French forces, and the intensity of operations diminished as peace negotiations got under way in Europe.

New Spain, too, was reinforced with metropolitan regiments. The process began with the transfer there of the America Regiment from 1764 to 1768, when it was relieved in Mexico City by Ultonia, Flandes and Saboya until 1771, 1772 and 1773 respectively. The Grenada Regiment was also in Vera Cruz from 1771 to 1784. The Asturias Regiment was stationed in Mexico City from 1777 to 1784, and Zamora in Vera Cruz from 1783 to 1789.

In Puerto Rico, the Leon Regiment served mostly at San Juan from 1766 until 1768, when it was relieved by Toledo until 1770. The Vitoria Regiment arrived in 1770, being joined by Bruselas in 1776, both regiments going back to Spain in 1783. Napoles arrived in 1784 and stayed until 1789–90, helping to form the new Fijo de Puerto Rico Regiment; thereafter Cantabria served in Puerto Rico from 1790 to 1798.

The 2nd Battalion of the metropolitan Toledo Regiment, part of which acted as marines on warships, was posted to Santo Domingo in 1781–82. In the latter year some 10,000 Spanish troops (Hibernia, Flandes, Aragon,

2nd Cataluna, Leon, Castillo de Campeche, Corona, Estramadura, Zamora, Soria, Guadalajara, Flandes, detachments of Santo Domingo and Havana, with artillery) gathered in various parts of the island for the intended invasion of Jamaica, but dispersed following the defeat of the French fleet at The Saints. The Leon Regiment remained at Guarico until 1783.

In Central America, elements of the Navarra and Hibernia regiments were in Honduras during 1782–83, while Corona was in Darien fighting local Indians. Units from Spain were also sent to Caracas and elsewhere in northern South America, but these postings must fall outside our study.

UNIFORMS & EQUIPMENT

REGULAR COLONIAL TROOPS, 1700–63

Following King Felipe V's accession, the senior army and navy officers posted "in the Indies" usually wore coats of the Bourbon family livery colors – blue, lined and cuffed with red, and garnished with gold buttons, lace or embroidery. Details were relatively vague until March 1760, when staff officers such as governors who did not have the rank of general were authorized blue coats and breeches with scarlet cuffs and waistcoats, with gold lace edging to the coat and waistcoat; a "king's lieutenant" (lieutenant-governor) and a town major had gold buttonholes (AGS, Guerra Moderna 2986).

To date, information on the early dress of the independent overseas companies and battalions is relatively sketchy; however, the information that has surfaced points to a generally similar uniform for nearly all the early North American colonial units up to the 1760s. Uniforms – or at least a consistent appearance of dress – do not seem to have been worn before the beginning of the 18th century. However, the troops sent from Spain in 1702 to take part in the relief of St Augustine from its British besiegers were said to wear uniforms, while the local regular troops in Fort San Marcos did not have such clothing. Even so, uniform dress was certainly being introduced at that time for regular troops.

The halberdier guards of the Viceroy of New Spain in Mexico City changed from the yellow livery of the Hapsburg kings to the blue and red uniforms of the Bourbon royal family soon after Felipe V's accession (see illustration on page 8). On 6 January 1703 the journal of Father Robles mentions that the soldiers of the viceroy's palace in Mexico City came out dressed in a new blue cloth uniform with scarlet cuffs and stockings, with "three-cornered hats such as those used in France." The previous September, Robles had also mentioned a soldier wearing his hair in a queue tied with a cord or ribbon. These entries and other sources show that French fashions were being readily accepted throughout the Spanish empire, and also indicate that the Bourbon kings' royal livery was chosen for the colors of the uniforms – blue coats with red cuffs and lining. The viceroy's palace infantry company wore a blue coat and breeches, scarlet cuffs and waistcoat, with silver buttons and cuff lace. The viceroy's horse-guard unit wore a blue coat and breeches, scarlet cuffs and waistcoat, with

Grenadiers of the Aragon (left) and Guadalajara (right) metropolitan infantry regiments, from a manuscript of 1769; elements of both regiments, and of Lisboa, were stationed in New Orleans, Louisiana, in 1779–80. All wear black bearskin caps and white coats.
Aragon – white collar, scarlet cuffs, waistcoat and breeches, gold buttons.
Guadalajara – white breeches, scarlet cuffs and waistcoat, silver buttons.
According to Clonard (VII: 239), Guadalajara had the peculiar regimental distinction of a red stock; from November 1763 stocks or cravats in the metropolitan army were ordered to be black for infantry, cavalry and dragoons, and white for the artillery. (Anne S.K. Brown Military Collection, Brown University Library, Providence, USA)

Colonel Esteban Miro, Fijo de Luisiana Regiment; he was colonel commanding the regiment from 15 February 1781, and also Governor of Louisiana 1782–91. This likeness was probably made in about 1782; his hat has the "triple alliance" cockade of red, white and black that was worn during the American War of Independence, especially by Spanish troops in North America. The silver-laced hat also had a non-regulation black or dark blue aigrette, rising from behind the cockades. Miro wears the Fijo de Luisiana Regt's white and blue uniform, the cuffs with the three laces indicating the rank of colonel, below an intertwined lace denoting his appointment as a brigadier – these are just visible at bottom left. (Print after portrait; private collection)

silver buttons and lace, red bandoliers and horse housings both laced with silver. This was almost the same uniform as that worn by the royal horse guards in Madrid and Paris. The Vera Cruz Dragoon company raised in 1727 had a blue uniform with scarlet cuffs and waistcoat, laced hat, blue cape with a red collar and, for warm weather, a linen uniform with red cuffs.

Detailed dress regulations appeared from 1731 for the marine battalion organized at Vera Cruz, which was to wear the same uniform as prescribed for marines in Spain under their dress regulations of 28 April 1717. Private soldiers were issued a blue cloth coat, waistcoat and breeches, with scarlet cuffs and scarlet lining of a lighter cloth, scarlet stockings, 36 gilt-brass buttons for the coat and 24 for the waistcoat, a hat edged with gold-colored lace, a white linen shirt and cravat, and black leather shoes. Corporals had one gold lace edging to the cuffs, and sergeants two. Drummers and fifers also wore the royal livery colors, their coats being garnished with livery lace – red with a central gold line, and edged each side with a violet line. This clothing was to be issued every 28 months. Furthermore, all soldiers, corporals, drummers and fifers had a "grenadier" cap of blue cloth, with a turn-up (almost certainly scarlet) in front, not made too high, and edged with fur that could be obtained from Pensacola in Florida (MN, Ms 2179).

Besides this cloth uniform, the troops serving at sea "and in warm climates" were issued a "a coat of strong linen," without lining and garnished with blue wool cloth buttonhole loops. There was one lace loop

Trooper of presidial cavalry, 1804. This somewhat naïve rendering shows the unusual dress and equipment of the Cuera cavalry in the 1790s and early 1800s. The blue jacket and breeches, red collar and cuffs, brass buttons, brimmed hat with a red ribbon band, shield, lance, pistols, *escopetta* carbine and ventral cartridge box were common to all Cuera troopers. The leather jacket is shown here as being waist length – possibly a later, or a regional, modification. In San Francisco, California, the soldier Amador recalled his leather coat as being "to the knee," and this shortened version may have been used only in the presidio garrisons further east. (Uniformes 81; Archivo General de Indias, Sevilla)

below the collar, three at the waist and three at each cuff, and the buttons were "of strong linen." A pair of linen breeches was also issued, along with shirts and cravats for this tropical uniform (AGS, Tesoro 18 and Hacienda 710).

The battalions formed at Cartagena de Indias in 1736, at Santo Domingo and Panama in 1738, the Corona Regiment at Vera Cruz in 1740, and Puerto Rico in 1741 all adopted basically the same uniform as the Vera Cruz battalion, with some variations. The most common difference for the cloth uniforms was the use of a scarlet waistcoat rather than blue. The regulations for the Cartagena de Indias and Panama battalions mention blue coats and breeches with other items in scarlet, all of a lightweight cloth, as well as the coat lining and a waistcoat of strong linen (AGI, Panama 355). In Puerto Rico, the 1741 regulation stated that "the clothing of the companies of infantry and artillery will be of blue wool cloth with red cuffs, red waistcoat and stockings of this color [red] …to be issued every 24 to 30 months" (AGI, Santo Domingo 2499). The linen clothing is hinted at, but not described. It is interesting to note that the uniforms for Puerto Rico were supplied from Vera Cruz, so the linen uniform may have been similar to that of the marine battalion there. By 1765, and certainly for some years previously, the Puerto Rico battalion's only uniform was of white "Bramante" linen with blue collar and cuffs and gold buttons (AGI, Santo Domingo 2501).

By the 1730s, and possibly before, troops stationed in Cuba and Florida had the same uniform. Conde de Clonard, in his 1850s *Historia Organica*, mentions white faced with red for the 1717 regiment formed at Havana, but so far this has not been confirmed by any primary archival document. The primary sources mention instead an obviously blue and red cloth uniform, as well as a linen hot-weather uniform. Amongst the material shipped to St Augustine, Florida, for clothing the garrison in 1735 was 1,029 ells of blue cloth, 196 ells of red, 400 pairs of stockings, hats laced with yellow silk, buttons and shoes. Much the same items were shipped to St Augustine in 1739, with even more blue and red cloth (see Plate A). There was also a large quantity of linen, obviously for hot-weather clothing (UFSC, AGI 58-2-4 and 58-1-34/64).

The uniform of the troops in Havana was much the same. A 1737 shipment there also mentions a lot of blue cloth, smaller quantities of red cloth, white linen shirts, black hats, and a large quantity of "good Bramante linen" (UFSC, AGI 87-1-2 60). Article 42 of the April 1753 regulations of the Havana Regiment – into which the garrison of Florida was merged – specified for the infantry a "blue cloth coat and breeches, red cuffs and waistcoat, in that cloth which is most adequate and proportionate to the station of that climate, red stockings, hat with its lace, and sword knot, which materials will have to be brought from Spain being of the better quality, appearance and longer lasting. And that [lace] of the sergeants will be with its distinctions on the coat cuffs and pocket flaps, that of the corporals at the cuffs, the musket slings, powder flask and belt

The provincial battalions of Pardos Libres of Puebla and Mexico City, organized in 1776 and 1777 respectively, both had the same uniform (at left). These "Free Brown" units wore a dark blue coat and breeches, with red collar, dark blue cuffs with red cuff flaps, white turnbacks, yellow metal buttons and hat lace, black gaiters and buff accoutrements. The soldier of the Tlaxcala y Puebla Provincial Regiment (at right) wears its dark blue coat, waistcoat and breeches, with scarlet collar and cuffs, yellow buttons and hat lace. The other provincial regiments were Mexico, Cordoba y Xalapa, Toluca, Oaxaca, Guadalajara and Mechoacan. (Archivo General de la Nacion, Mexico City)

Colonel Serbando Gomez de la Cortina, Count Cortina, of the Mexico City Urban Infantry Regiment, 1781. Raised in 1693, this was the most prestigious militia regiment in New Spain, counting among its members some of the wealthiest men in Mexico City. The uniform was a scarlet coat and breeches, with blue collar, cuffs and waistcoat, white coat lining, gold buttons and lace, and white stockings. From the white cape with the red cross spread on the table, the colonel was also a knight of the Order of Santiago. (Museo Nacional de Historia, Mexico City)

of white leather and the same for the cartridge box." (For the artillery companies, see Plate A3; the cavalry uniform was not specified.) On the whole, this regulation confirmed the uniform in use by colonial troops defending the Spanish Main before 1763, i.e. blue, faced with scarlet, except for a few artillery companies.

Regular colonial troops, 1764–93

In general, the uniforms followed closely the styles of the Spanish metropolitan army. Unlike the line infantry troops in Spain, who mostly wore white waistcoats and breeches from 1791, the colonial units' waistcoats and breeches were often of various colors until later than that. The "Roman"-style black helmet with a crest worn in Spain from 1775 to 1782 was not used by units in North America.

The Espana Dragoon Regiment, raised in New Spain during 1764, wore a blue coat, breeches and cape, with scarlet collar and cuffs, white metal buttons on both side of the coat's breast, and a silver-laced hat. For the Mexico Dragoon Regiment raised in 1765, see the illustration on page 9.

The Corona Regiment of New Spain was attached as the 3rd Battalion of the America Regiment between 1765 and 1768, and wore its uniform – a blue coat and breeches, with yellow collar, cuffs and waistcoat, white metal buttons and white hat lace. The facings changed from yellow to red from 1768, when the Corona became fully autonomous from the America Regiment. For the regiments of Nueva Espana, Mexico and Puebla raised in 1788, see the illustration on page 10.

The Catalonian Volunteers wore the peculiar dress of Spanish mountain troops (see Plate C3). The veterans in the Corps of "Invalidos" had a blue uniform with scarlet collar, cuffs and waistcoat and silver buttons in 1771. From 1773, they had a blue uniform including the cuffs and waistcoat, with a white collar, and gold buttons later changed to silver. The two dragoon companies on the island of Carmen from 1773 were uniformed in a blue coat, breeches and cape, with scarlet cuffs, lapels and waistcoat, and silver buttons. The infantry companies there had almost the same uniform, with a scarlet collar and gold buttons, but without the red lapels or the cape. The 1773 Acapulco company had a white uniform with scarlet collar and cuffs and white metal buttons. The two companies at San Juan de Ulloa from 1780 had a blue coat and breeches, yellow collar, cuffs and waistcoat, and white metal buttons. The 1788 San Blas company wore a short blue coat with yellow collar and cuffs, white metal buttons, white turnbacks, waistcoat and gaiter-trousers, and a plain unlaced hat. The 1792 Vera Cruz Battalion had a sky-blue coat with scarlet cuffs and lapels, white linen waistcoat and breeches, and a round hat.

In Yucatan and Central America, the 1754 Castilla de Campeche Battalion wore blue cloth uniform with scarlet collar, cuffs and waistcoat, gold buttons and hat lace; they also had a linen uniform with scarlet collar and cuffs and gold buttons, which, by the 1770s, appears to have become their only uniform. The Bacalar company had a similar uniform. The Yucatan Dragoons wore blue with scarlet cuffs and waistcoat, silver buttons and hat lace, and also had a white linen uniform with scarlet facings (and white collar). For the Fijo de Guatemala Regiment, see Plate G3. The 1786 Omoa company had a white linen uniform with scarlet collar, cuffs and lace.

In Cuba, the reorganized Havana Regiment continued to wear its blue and red uniform until 1769 (see Plate E1). The dragoons were re-raised as the America Dragoons, initially wearing a white Bramante linen uniform faced with yellow and trimmed with yellow buttonhole lace. From 1769 they had a cloth uniform consisting of a yellow coat, breeches and cape, with blue collar and cuffs, a blue waistcoat (with yellow lapels?), white metal buttons and white hat lace. The Cuba Infantry Regiment organized in 1788–89 wore a white coat with violet cuffs and lapels but a green collar and piping, white turnbacks, brass buttons, a white waistcoat and breeches, and yellow hat lace.

The Santo Domingo Battalion had, from 1771 and probably for some years previously, a white linen uniform with collar and cuffs of "*lila*" (here seemingly a shade of blue – a full blue was worn by the 1780s), silver buttons and hat lace (AGI, Santo Domingo 1097). The "Fieles Practicos" border company had a short blue jacket and blue breeches, red lapels, a white waistcoat and stockings and a black round hat. The Fijo de Puerto Rico Regiment raised in 1790 had a white uniform with blue collar, cuffs and lapels and white metal buttons; its peculiar lapels each had only three large buttons at the top, center and bottom.

The "Cuera soldiers"

The arms and equipment, and eventually the uniforms of these troops are among the most unusual to be found in the annals of military history. The influences of the Indians, the North African Moors, as well as peculiarly Iberian features and even those of the Bourbon dynasty were all to be found when one looked at fully equipped soldier. He wore a "*cuera*" (leather jacket), was armed with a sword, pistols and either a musket or, more commonly, a lance, and carried a bull-hide shield called an "*adarga*" for protection (see Plates B1 and B2, and the illustrations).

Cavalry of the Provincial Mixed Legion of San Carlos, New Spain, 1771. Raised from 1767, the legion had 49 cavalry companies and nine infantry companies by the 1780s. The illustration shows a white felt hat with red tuft, a blue poncho with red edging worn over a short blue coat with yellow facings and white metal buttons, with buff breeches, laced black gaiters and black shoes. Note the musket carried on the right side, and the drawn sword. A plate of the contemporaneous Provincial Mixed Legion of Principe shows much the same uniform, but with a red collar, lapels and cuffs to the blue coat, and a blue waistcoat. (Archivo Generale de la Nacion, Mexico City)

Captain Pierre Rousseau of the Louisiana Militia, c.1782. He wears a dark blue coat and breeches, with scarlet collar, cuffs, lapels and waistcoat, gold buttons and epaulets, and gold lace edging the waistcoat and the hat. Note the "triple alliance" cockade: red for Spain at left, black for the USA at center, and white for France at right. (Louisiana State Museum, New Orleans)

In November 1727, Brigadier de Rivera noted that the garrison at Bahia de Espiritu Santo, Texas, paid "special attention to the soldier's uniforms," but unfortunately he did not describe them. Article 64 of the 1729 regulations made it clear that all soldiers were to be "uniformly dressed in the usual uniform of the same color." These regulations also listed the "provisions, equipment, and other necessities that must be provided for the soldiers"; blue and red cloth figured, along with black hats, leather military jackets, accoutrements, weapons and horse equipment. By then, dragoon-style leather gaiters, laced or buckled at the sides and worn over low boots or shoes, seem to have been in general use. The regulations make clear that there was a uniform for the "Cuera" cavalry from the early 18th century, and that it was blue and red (AGI, Guadalajara 144).

However, not everyone on the frontier was in uniform, as was noted by the Marquis de Rubi during his 1766–67 inspection. At El Pasage in May that year, the clothing was somewhat uniform, being blue with scarlet breeches and adorned with silver and gold lace or embroidery. At Guajoquilla in late May, each soldier dressed to his own taste or means. At El Paso in July, the marquis noted that the clothing was in "a deplorable state and not uniform," the leather jackets being too thin and thus useless against arrows. Moving on to Janos in October, he again found some equipment wanting, notably poorly-made leather jackets; "the costumes were not uniform for all the clothing of the company," but scarlet cloth was mentioned for lapels and blue cloth for breeches. At Monclova in June 1767 the marquis finally saw what he considered to be a well-clothed company, all wearing a short blue coat with scarlet cuffs, silver buttons and a scarlet waistcoat (AGI, Guadalajara 272).

Probably the best-known document on the Cuera cavalry is the regulation of 10 September 1772 (see Plate B2). There is evidence suggesting that by a few years later this simple 1772 "blue short jacket with a red collar and red cuffs" had red lapels in some cases. In 1779 the uniform and equipment of the troops at San Antonio, Texas, was described in detail. Each soldier had a blue short jacket with red collar, cuffs and lapels, a red waistcoat, blue breeches, 48 large gilt buttons for the jacket and breeches, 18 small gilt buttons for the waistcoat, a cape, a hat, a black cravat, shirts, drawers, dragoon-style gaiters and boots (AGI, Guadalajara 283). Armament consisted of a type of light musket called an *escopeta* with a sturdy miquelet-type lock, a pair of pistols, a sword with sword knot and sword belt, a lance, a shield, a leather jacket, a cartridge box holding 24 rounds, and a bandoleer that was presumably embroidered with the name "San Antonio." A complete set of horse equipment was listed, along with seven horses (including presumably a colt) and a mule.

Second lieutenant Michel Dragon, Louisiana Militia, in a portrait by J. Salazar, c.1793–95. A native of Athens, Greece, Dragon joined the militia as a private in 1771, and rose to be commissioned on 12 February 1792. He is portrayed wearing the new militia uniform decreed for all the Spanish colonies on 1 January 1792, which in the case of the Louisiana Militia simply meant the addition of a gold lace edging to the scarlet collar of the blue coat, and substituting white waistcoats and breeches for the old scarlet waistcoats and blue breeches. (Louisiana State Museum, New Orleans)

(continued on page 33)

FLORIDA & WEST INDIES, c.1730s–1763
1: Infantry private, 1735–40
2: Infantry officer, c.1740
3: Artillery gunner, c.1755

1

2

3

A

THE NORTHERN INTERIOR PROVINCES
1: Trooper, Cuera cavalry, mid 18th C
2: Trooper, Cuera cavalry, as 1772 regulations
3: Trooper, Cuera cavalry, undress uniform, c.1780s

B

CALIFORNIA & NORTHWEST COAST, 1769–1790s
1: Officer, Cuera cavalry, undress, 1780
2: Trooper, Ligera cavalry, c 1778–83
3: Private, Catalonian Volunteer companies, c.1767–94

C

COLONIAL TROOPS, LOUISIANA, 1769–1780s
1: Private, Luisiana Regiment, c.1780
2: Officer, St Louis militia cavalry, 1779
3: Officer, New Orleans militia battalion, c.1780

D

COLONIAL TROOPS, LOUISIANA & FLORIDA, 1769–1780s
1: Grenadier, Havana Regiment, 1769–86
2: Drummer, Luisiana Regiment, 1770s–80s
3: Private, Luisiana Dragoon company, 1780s

E

METROPOLITAN TROOPS, LOUISIANA & FLORIDA, 1770s–80s
1: First sergeant, fusilier company, Toledo Regiment
2: Private, fusilier company, Hibernia Regiment
3: Grenadier, Rey Regiment

F

METROPOLITAN TROOPS, LOUISIANA, FLORIDA & CENTRAL AMERICA, 1770s–80s
1: Private, Espana Regiment
2: Private, fusilier company, Principe Regiment, c.1775–82
3: Captain, Fijo de Guatemala Regiment

G

DRAGOONS, ENGINEERS & ARTILLERY, 1770s–80s
1: Private, Guatemala Dragoons, c.1779–82
2: Officer, Royal Corps of Engineers, c.1770
3: Gunner, Royal Corps of Artillery

H

Orders issued on 21 September 1780 by the Commandant-General of the Interior Provinces left no doubt as to lapels and other details. The uniform of the enlisted men was to be a blue short coat with scarlet collar, cuffs and lapels, gold buttons, linen or chamois waistcoat, blue breeches, and a blue cloth cape, with a poncho that also covered the soldier and his weapons against the hot sun or rain. The black hat was to have the brim turned up on the left side and held with a loop, "so as to handle the musket with ease," and a red wool plume. The sword was not to vary in length and was to be carried from a swordbelt around the waist when mounted; when on foot, the belt was worn diagonally over the right shoulder. The leather jacket, shield, and other equipment were retained, but the bandoleer was not to be supplied in future, as it was considered useless (BLCA 15: IV). According to these 1780 instructions, the officers had two types of uniforms, for dress and undress (see Plate C1).

The orders of the commandant-general were not applied everywhere, however, and only a year later, in 1781, the uniforms intended for the California peninsula were without lapels, and equipment included the bandoleers bearing the embroidered name of the presidio, exactly as specified in 1772. In December 1794, the uniform of the non-commissioned officers and privates was officially changed back to its original form: in future tailors were ordered to make the jackets "with scarlet cuffs and collars only" and to "omit the lapels" (BLCA 7, XII). This did not affect the dress uniform of the officers, but their undress uniform also lost its lapels – though not the two gold laces on the collar. The buff waistcoat of the 1780 regulations does not seem to have caught on, at least not in California, where one notes scarlet or blue waistcoats.

Trooper, Puerto Rico Militia Cavalry, 1785; watercolor by José Campeche. There were five companies, one in San Juan and the others active in various towns. The uniform consisted of a white coat, waistcoat and breeches, with scarlet collar, cuffs and lapels, blue buttonhole lace, gold buttons and hat lace, buff accoutrements, and scarlet housings edged with yellow lace. (Uniforme 112; Archivo General de Indias, Sevilla)

MILITIA UNITS, pre–1763

The wear of uniform dress by militiamen was not common in the Spanish overseas empire before the 1760s. Well-to-do volunteers in Mexico City may have been among the first to adopt uniforms, possibly during the first half of the 18th century. By the 1750s the city's uniformed companies were organized by trade and artisan corporations. The Silversmith's Company and the Commerce Regiment were the senior units, and wore scarlet uniforms faced with blue (see illustrations, pages 14 & 22). Most others had white or gray-white coats with red cuffs and waistcoats, and, according to

Puerto Rico Militia infantry, 1785, in a watercolor by José Campeche. In 1778 some 18 companies of white militiamen (left) were at various towns on the island; San Juan, Ponce and several other places had two companies each. The infantry's uniform was a white coat, waistcoat and breeches, with scarlet collar, cuffs and buttonhole lace on the front, gold buttons and hat lace, and buff accoutrements.
The Puerto Rico Moreno infantry (right) mustered free Africans, mostly in San Juan. Its uniform was a black cap with a brass badge bearing the royal arms; this ample blue *gambeta* coat with red collar and cuffs; a red jacket or sleeved waistcoat with blue collar and cuffs, white metal buttons and white buttonhole lace; white breeches, and buff accoutrements. The buttons have sometimes been shown as gold, but the 1775 clothing contract for this uniform and the inspection reports all state white metal (AGS, Tesoro 25, leg 17; AGI, Santo Domingo 2507; Uniformes 113 & 114, Archivo General de Indias, Sevilla)

drawings in New York Public Library's Vinkhuisen Collection, a few wore blue faced with red. Some of the militia units that assembled from various parts of eastern New Spain in late 1762 to defend Vera Cruz against the rumored British attack had various uniforms. The Cholula companies had a cotton coat, presumably white, with scarlet collar, cuffs and waistcoat. The Valladolid "Spanish" companies wore blue coats, and the Pardos had cotton coats, both with yellow facings. Most units – and there were mounted companies – wore local civilian "*vestuario de manga*" that mainly consisted of capes, ponchos and brimmed hats.

There is not much evidence of uniforms being used by many militiamen elsewhere. Even in 1760 in Havana, Ribera's description lamented that uniforms were not mandatory, and argued that militia officers should be required to attend parades with their swords and spontoons.

Militia units from 1763

This situation changed drastically from 1763. The sweeping reforms in the imperial defense system also imposed uniforms on a vast number of urban and provincial (rural) militiamen. In some cases, for instance in 1775 for Puerto Rico, uniforms were made in Spain for issue to the island's "disciplined militia" units. The militia of Cuba were the first to be governed by detailed regulations, first issued on 17 June 1764 and printed in 1769; these specified uniforms and colors for all disciplined units (AGI, Santo Domingo 2078). Infantry units had white uniforms. The Havana Blancos Battalion had black facings with silver buttons, the Cuba Blancos Battalion red facings and gold buttons, the Puerto Principe Battalion black and gold respectively, and the Cuatro Villas Battalion blue and silver, all featuring six lace loops on the coat front (see page 12). The Matanzas Battalion had blue collar and cuffs, white cuff flap, gold buttons and lace. The Havana Volunteer Cavalry Regiment wore blue with scarlet collar, cuffs and lapels and gold buttons, as well as a white lightweight "Bramante"-fabric uniform with blue collar, cuffs and lapels. The Métis and free African companies were also assigned generally similar uniforms: the Havana Pardos Battalion wore white with green facings and gold buttons, the Cuba y Bayamo Pardos Battalion the same with silver buttons, and the Havana Morenos Libres Battalion a red, fully trimmed jacket/waistcoat, a blue coat and a black cap (see illustration of Puerto Rico Morenos, this page).

As with many other aspects of the 1764–69 Cuban regulations, the uniforms they prescribed were to some extent adopted by units in certain other colonies. The regulations of 17 May 1765 for the Puerto Rico militia (AGI, Santo Domingo, 2395, 2396) featured a white linen uniform with red facings and gold buttons for all 18 white infantry and five cavalry companies, the Moreno Company at San Juan having the same as its Havana counterpart. The 1767 Vera Cruz Militia regulations specified blue uniforms with scarlet collar, cuffs and waistcoats and gold buttons for its Blancos Battalion, but white faced with green and gold buttons for the Pardos Company, and the red jacket, blue coat

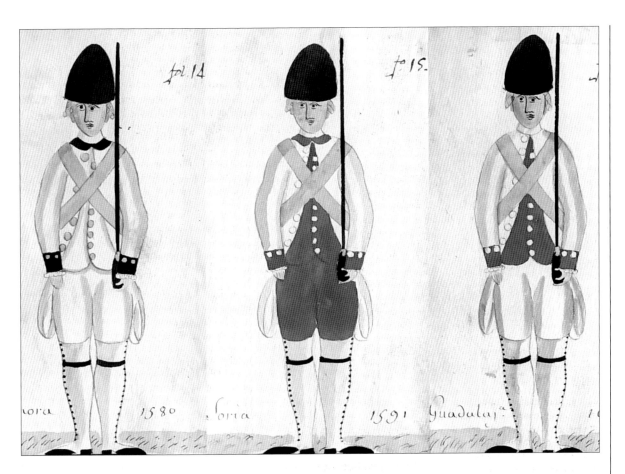

and black cap for the Morenos Company (AGN, Guerra Indiferente 40-B). The Santo Domingo militia was also dressed according to the same general pattern from 1769: white uniforms, with red collar and cuffs for the 12 Voluntarios Blanco infantry companies, and blue collar, cuffs and lapels for the six cavalry companies. The three free African Morenos companies were somewhat different, having a long red coat with black collar, cuffs and turnbacks, a red stock, white waistcoat, breeches and stockings, and a round hat laced white.

From 1770, the Louisiana militia infantry had a uniform of blue faced with scarlet, the coats of the gunners having no lapels, while the volunteer cavalrymen showed more variety (see illustration on page 45, and Plate D2). Insofar as uniforms were concerned, Louisiana did not follow the Cuban militia regulations. Some secondary sources mention unreferenced white uniforms with various facing colors for free African and Pardos infantry companies; none of the reports seen in archival documents mention these peculiar uniforms, and we must presently conclude that their dress was blue faced with red like other militiamen. These were the uniform colors of most militias in Louisiana, and Florida after 1783. The exceptions were the cavalry troops mentioned above, and the four companies of Voluntarios de Mississippi organized in 1792; the latter had a violet coat with white collar, cuffs and lapels, and gold buttons and buttonhole lace (AGI, Cuba 1441) – assuming, of course, that they already had their uniforms by the time the 1 January 1792 royal order arrived in Louisiana (see below).

Grenadiers of the Zamora, Soria and Guadalajara metropolitan infantry regiments, from a manuscript of 1780; all were present at the capture of Pensacola from the British the following year. All have black bearskin caps, buff accoutrements and white gaiters: Zamora – white uniform, black collar and cuffs, gold buttons. Soria – white coat, scarlet collar, cuffs, waistcoat and breeches, silver buttons. Guadalajara – white coat and breeches, scarlet cuffs and waistcoat, silver buttons. (Anne S.K. Brown Military Collection, Brown University Library, Providence, USA)

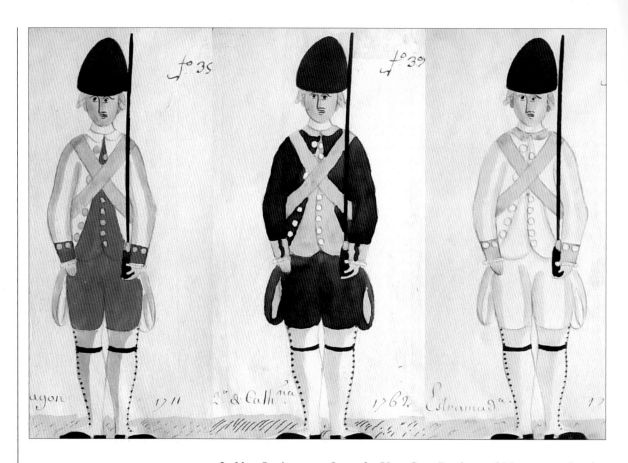

Grenadiers of the Aragon, 2nd Cataluna and Extremadura regiments, from a manuscript of 1780; again, all three were at the capture of Pensacola in 1781, and all have black bearskin caps, buff accoutrements and white gaiters:
Aragon – white coat and collar, scarlet cuffs, waistcoat and breeches, gold buttons.
2nd Catalonian – blue coat, cuff flap and breeches, yellow collar, cuffs, turnbacks and waistcoat, silver buttons.
Extremadura – white uniform with yellow collar and cuffs, silver buttons.
(Anne S.K. Brown Military Collection, Brown University Library, Providence, USA)

In New Spain, apart from the Vera Cruz Pardos and Morenos units, the color taken into wear during the 1760s by the disciplined provincial and urban militia units was usually blue, both for infantry and mounted units. The facings for units of militiamen of Spanish ancestry were usually scarlet, although other facing colors might be seen. It is impossible to describe the uniforms of the dozens of regiments in this small volume, and the reader is referred to the accompanying illustrations for a few examples of New Spain's militiamen. Not all had full blue cloth uniforms. In 1771, some cavalry troopers of the Principe Legion were reported wearing simply a "blue cloak [or poncho] with a badge bearing the royal arms… on the left side, a white hat with the [left] brim turned up [and held] by a scarlet cockade" (AGN, Virreyes 18). During September 1780, the Battalion of Acapulco and the Navidad Coast on the Pacific received a white linen coat, waistcoat and breeches with scarlet collar and cuffs, brass buttons and yellow hat lace. On the Atlantic coast, a lancer squadron of the Mexico Provincial Regiment patrolled "dressed uniformly in sleeved vests of blue cloth, edged with yellow, a black hat with [scarlet] cockade, and armed with lances, half-moons [small shields ?] and machetes" (AGN, Guerra Indiferente 65).

In the northern border provinces, from Texas to California, the dress of the militia was the same as that of the regular cavalry posted in the presidios except for white metal buttons. A regulation of 14 October 1778 for the province of Nueva Vizcaya specified a blue short coat and breeches, scarlet collar, cuffs and lapels, white metal buttons, black hat, blue cape, and arms and equipment like the light cavalry troopers (AGI, Guadalajara 270).

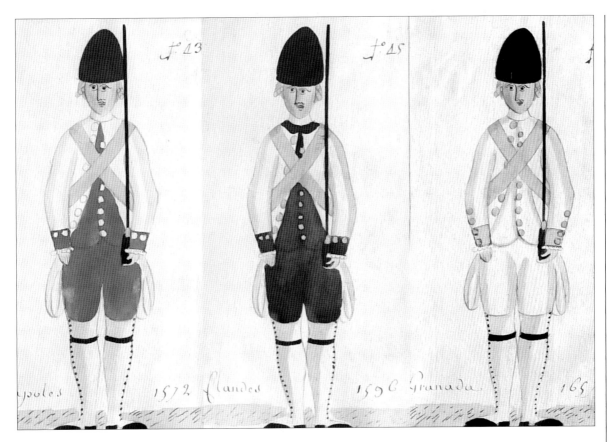

In Yucatan, the militia had white linen uniforms. The Campeche Blancos Battalion had blue collar, cuffs and breeches and silver buttons; the Merida Blancos Battalion had "lilac-red" collar and cuffs with gold buttons; the Yucatan Pardos Battalion had yellow collar and cuffs, and the Tiradores Pardos company yellow lapels and cuffs, with leather buttons. The militiamen of the urban companies organized in many towns from 1778 needed only the red cockade with a green leaf on their headgear, while the officers had white uniforms with, possibly, red or blue facings for Spanish-ancestry companies and yellow for other units, with silver-laced hats. In 1768 the Guatemala militia regulation, which applied to all of Central America, prescribed for the infantry a blue uniform with red cuffs and waistcoat, and officers were to have gold-laced hats and white stockings; see Plate H1 for cavalry. Apart from the "disciplined militia" units, the bulk of militiamen served in their own everyday clothing.

From the 1760s, the militia artillery was assigned the same uniform as the regular artillery (see Plate H3), though differences in detail were sometimes noted. For example, the Louisiana artillery company raised in 1778 did not have gold lace on its uniform.

The 1789 and 1792 militia regulations
During the 1780s, it was felt that the various militia uniforms throughout the Empire needed to be standardized. On 7 March 1789 the provincial militia uniform was henceforth decreed to be of a "bark color," while the urban militia would have a "brown color." Facings were to be scarlet collars, cuffs and lapels with gold buttons for the provincial militia,

From the same 1780 manuscript, grenadiers of three more metropolitan regiments, all wearing black bearskin caps, white coats and gaiters, and buff accoutrements. Napoles and Flandes were at the capture of Pensacola, and Grenada was posted to Vera Cruz: Napoles – scarlet cuffs, waistcoat and breeches, silver buttons. Flandes – blue collar, cuffs, waistcoat and breeches, gold buttons. Grenada – white uniform, green cuffs, gold buttons. (Anne S.K. Brown Military Collection, Brown University Library, Providence, USA)

and the same without the lapels for the urban militia. This instruction was not greeted with enthusiasm, and few militiamen in the New World adopted it. Faced with this resistance, the authorities in Spain revised the requirements so as to have, on the whole, the same colors as worn by the metropolitan Spanish militia. On 1 January 1792, the uniform for all the militias in the Spanish colonies was established: for infantry units, a blue coat with red collar, cuffs and lapels, white turnbacks, gold buttons, and a gold-lace edging to the collar; for cavalry, the same but with silver buttons and silver collar lace. The waistcoat and breeches were white.

METROPOLITAN REGIMENTS, 1726–63

In general, metropolitan troops sent to North America had similar uniforms to those worn in Spain. Contracts for infantry uniforms during the 1730s and 1740s generally specified a white cloth coat and breeches, the coat with 30 buttons and lined with light cloth or linen, with cloth cuffs and a waistcoat of the facing color, 24 waistcoat buttons, linen lining for the waistcoat and breeches, a white shirt, a cravat, a pair of stockings, a pair of shoes, and a hat edged with lace of the regimental button color (AGS, Hacienda 710, Guerra Moderna 5356-5362). Until the 1740s stockings for NCOs and enlisted men were usually of the facing color. White gaiters appear to have become standard issue from the early 1740s.

The facing, and button and lace colors, for infantry regiments sent entirely or in part to America were as follows, where known:

Africa – blue
Aragon – red; gold (1740s), silver (1762)
Asturias – yellow (1738), red (1743), blue (1747); gold (1740s), silver (1761)
Cantabria – blue; silver
Cataluna – red; silver
Espana – green; silver (1740s), gold (1762)
Grenada – green; gold
Lisboa – red; silver (1740s), gold (1762)
Murcia – blue; silver
Navarra – red; gold
Portugal – red
Sevilla – blue; silver
Toledo – blue; gold
Valencia – blue; silver

For drummers and fifers, see the illustration on page 16 and Plate E2. Regimental field and fusilier officers were armed with a sword and a spontoon, sergeants with a sword and a halberd; the polearms were 6ft 6in high. Grenadier officers and NCOs were armed with a hanger and a musket with its bayonet.

During the 1740s, the Almanza Dragoons in Cuba had a yellow coat and breeches, blue cuffs and waistcoat, 46 silver coat buttons and 43 waistcoat buttons, a yellow cape, a hat laced with white, laced gaiters and short boots, a white shirt, a black cravat, and blue housings edged white (AGS, Hacienda 710). The Italica Dragoons had a similar uniform, but with black cuffs, yellow waistcoat and silver buttons. The Edimburgo Dragoons in Havana during 1762 wore a yellow coat and breeches, with blue collar, cuffs and waistcoat, silver buttons and white hat lace. Until March 1760 dragoon trumpeters usually wore the reversed colors of their regimental uniform; thereafter, they wore the blue and scarlet royal uniform trimmed with the king's livery lace.

Metropolitan regiments, 1764–93

Although the 1770–82 "Roman"-style black cap worn in Spain was not used by metropolitan units sent to North America, grenadiers had their fur caps even in the most torrid stations. The regiments are listed below under their stations:

Rank distinctions, post-1768: Lt Ignacio de Balderas of the colonial Fijo de Luisiana Regiment, c.1790, in a portrait by J. Salazar. His white coat, worn over a blue waistcoat, has a blue collar, cuffs and lining, with silver buttons and the single right epaulet of this rank. His hat is edged with silver lace and bears the scarlet national cockade, and he has a silver-hilted sword. Balderas joined the regiment as a private in 1771 at the age of 14; reported as intelligent and zealous, he rose through the ranks, being commissioned second-lieutenant in February 1781, lieutenant in October 1787, and captain in 1798. (Louisiana State Museum, New Orleans)

Cuba
Cordoba (1763–65) – White coat and breeches, green collar, cuffs and waistcoat, gold buttons.

Lisboa (1765–69) – White uniform, scarlet cuffs, gold buttons.

Sevilla (1770) – White uniform, black cuffs, gold buttons.

Irlanda (1771) – Red coat and breeches, blue waistcoat and cuffs, gold buttons.

Aragon (1771–74) – see page 17. The 1769 army list further notes six buttons on the pocket flaps and three on the cuffs.

Guadalajara (1770–74) – White coat and breeches, scarlet cuffs and waistcoat, gold buttons.

Principe (1771–82)– see Plate G2.

Navarra (1779–83) – see page 46.

New Spain
America (1764–68) – Blue coat and breeches, yellow collar, cuffs and waistcoat, silver buttons.

Saboya (1768–73) – White coat, waistcoat and breeches, black collar and cuffs, silver buttons.

Flandes (1768–72) – White coat and breeches, blue collar, cuffs, waistcoat and breeches, gold buttons.

Ultonia (1768–71) – Red coat, waistcoat and breeches, black collar and cuffs, gold buttons (AGN, H 165).

Grenada (1771–84) – White uniform, green cuffs, gold buttons.

Asturias (1777–84) – White coat and breeches, blue waistcoat and cuffs, gold buttons.

Zamora (1783–89) – see page 35.

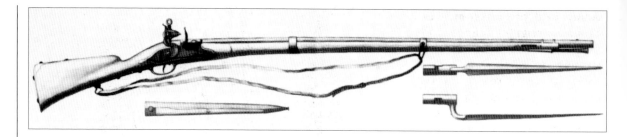

Model 1757 infantry musket, the standard firearm for foot troops that was widely used by regulars and militia units in Spain and its empire until the 1790s/early 1800s. It had brass furnishings including three barrel-bands; the length was 4.9 English feet (1.5m), and that of the triangular-section socket bayonet 1.6ft (0.49m) – the bayonet scabbard is also shown below. (Print after Tomas de Morla's *Tratado de Artilleria*, 1803)

Louisiana 1769–1770
Lisboa, Aragon and Guadalajara – see under Cuba above.
Louisiana & W. Florida 1779–83 campaigns
See Plates F & G for metropolitan uniforms.
Puerto Rico
Leon (1766–68) – White coat and breeches, scarlet collar, cuffs and
    waistcoat, silver buttons.
Toledo (1768–70) – White coat and cuff flap, blue collar, cuffs, waistcoat
    and breeches, gold buttons.
Vitoria (1770–83) – White coat and collar, scarlet cuffs, waistcoat and
    breeches, silver buttons.
Brusselas (1776–83) – White uniform, no collar, blue cuffs,
    silver buttons.
Napoles (1784–90) – White coat, scarlet cuffs, waistcoat and breeches,
    silver buttons.
Cantabria (1790–98) – White uniform, scarlet collar, cuffs, lapels
    (from 1791) edged with sky-blue piping, silver buttons.
Santo Domingo
Toledo (1781–82) – see page 18.

Rank distinctions
Officers and NCOs did not display rank distinctions on their uniforms before 1768, but often carried varnished wooden canes that indicated rank. A colonel's cane had a large gold pommel, a lieutenant-colonel's the same in silver, the major's and captain's canes a small silver pommel, the lieutenant's and chaplain's an ivory pommel, and the sub-lieutenant's a wooden pommel with a silver ring. Quartermasters had a wooden pommel, sergeants a plain wooden cane, and corporals a thinner cane. All officers' canes had loops of silver cord except for the colonels', which had gold cords; those of the NCOs had fabric or leather cords.

From 1768, officers' ranks were indicated by lines of cuff lace, or epaulets, of gold or silver according to their unit's button color. A colonel had three laces around each cuff, a lieutenant-colonel two, and a major (*sargento mayor*) had one; these field-grade officers had no epaulets, and continued to carry a cane. A captain had an epaulet on each shoulder, a lieutenant one on the right shoulder, and a sub-lieutenant one on the left shoulder. When on duty, e.g. serving as officer of the guard, all officer ranks wore at the throat a gorget, a gilded crescent with a centered silver badge bearing the arms of Spain. Sergeants had epaulets in their unit's facing color: a first sergeant an epaulet on each shoulder, and a sergeant one on the right only. Corporals had lace edging to the top of their cuffs. Officer cadets attached to a unit wore its uniform with an aiguillette of the button color on the right shoulder.

Arms and accoutrements

From the reign of Felipe V the weapons and equipment were strongly influenced by those used in the French Army; indeed, during the War of the Spanish Succession stocks were imported from France, and were then copied by Spanish manufacturers.

At the beginning of the 18th century a regular soldier in the Spanish Indies was usually armed like his counterpart in Europe: a musket with its bayonet, and a sword (or a saber for a grenadier). Some soldiers may still have carried matchlocks and plug bayonets, but these were eventually replaced by flintlock muskets with socket bayonets. At this time the calibers and models of Spanish military firearms were not yet standardized.

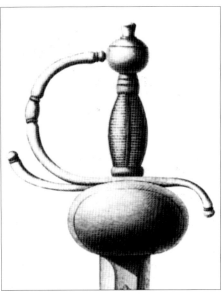

ABOVE LEFT **Head of officer's Model 1728 spontoon, introduced by a royal order of 12 September that year; the total length of this weapon was 6.9ft (2.1 metres). French-style spontoons had been in Spanish Army use since 1704. (Print after Tomas de Morla's *Tratado de Artilleria*, 1803)**

ABOVE RIGHT **Hilt of cavalry broadsword, Model 1728. This sturdy weapon had an elegant design somewhat reminiscent of the 17th century, and featured an elaborate steel guard and a straight blade 36in (0.91m) long. Several examples of this popular weapon have been found in the American southwest. (Print after Tomas de Morla's 1803 *Tratado de Artilleria*)**

In 1702, when the War of the Spanish Succession broke out, a standard caliber of 16 balls to the pound weight (approximately 18.5mm) was adopted for infantry and dragoon muskets to conform with French Army weapons, some of which were sent to Spain and its colonies, and this remained unchanged for the rest of the 18th century. The first standard model infantry musket was introduced in 1717 – the same year that France introduced its first standard weapon. It is generally believed that both models had many similarities, such as the barrel being secured to the stock by pins, and the furnishings being made of polished steel; its single steel barrel-band was for the attachment of the buff sling.

In June 1757 a new Spanish infantry musket appeared, distinguished by its barrel-bands, and by brass furnishings. This weapon was widely manufactured and remained the standard regulation musket used in Spain and overseas until the 1790s. Cavalry carbines had the same caliber, but featured brass furnishings from at least the 1720s. Pistols were mounted in brass, and usually had the same caliber.

Following the War of the Spanish Succession, swords for privates and corporals were no longer issued in metropolitan infantry units, but they continued to be worn by soldiers in the regular colonial units, apparently until after the Seven Years' War. NCOs and officers continued to have swords, and grenadiers had sabers.

In the early 1700s, the equipment used by Spanish troops was generally similar to that of the French Army. Until the late 1730s this consisted of a ventral ("belly") cartridge box, usually holding nine rounds, slung on the buff sword belt, and a hardwood or horn powder flask trimmed with brass and slung over the shoulder on a narrow buff strap. Grenadiers had an additional large pouch to hold grenades as well as cartridges, carried on a wide buff shoulder belt upon which a brass matchcase was fixed. In 1736 the French infantry changed to a larger cartridge box or *giberne*

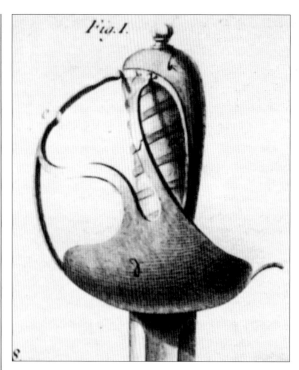

Hilt of dragoon saber, Model 1768, featuring a steel guard that gave good protection to the hand. The straight blade was about 38in (0.96m) long. (Print after Tomas de Morla's *Tratado de Artilleria*, 1803)

suspended by a buff shoulder belt, and thereafter the Spanish line infantry gradually adopted this; however, the ventral box continued to be used as well, both types sometimes being shown in use together.

Tacolli's 1759 manuscript shows only the shoulder cartridge box; however, by about 1761–63 an enlarged ventral cartridge box of reddish leather, holding 55 to 60 rounds, was worn on the buff waist belt to the right of the bayonet scabbard, with the powder horn hanging from its narrow sling over the left shoulder. From 1768 the equipment was changed to a black leather cartridge box holding 29 rounds, and a bayonet, carried on two crossed buff shoulder belts with open brass buckles. From about 1778–80, and certainly by 1784, grenadiers wore the same type of cartridge boxes as the fusiliers, and their now pointless brass matchcases were gradually discarded except for decorative purposes. The belts were buff until the late 1780s, when they were pipeclayed white.

Until 1768 infantry officers were armed with a spontoon and a sword, sergeants with a halberd and a sword. Thereafter infantry company officers carried a musket with its bayonet, as well as a sword (or saber for grenadier officers). The cartridge box, and the sword and bayonet, each hung from their own shoulder belt; these were quite ornate, usually being covered with silken material in the unit's facing color and edged with regimental lace. Infantry sergeants' halberds were also replaced by muskets with bayonets, cartridge boxes and buff accoutrements from 1768.

In theory, dragoons were mounted infantry, but in fact they often acted as cavalry; they were armed with a saber, a long musket and pistols. A trooper of the heavy cavalry was armed with a heavy, straight-bladed sword, a carbine and a pair of pistols. Dragoons and cavalrymen had a wide shoulder belt to hold the musket or carbine on their right side, and a small cartridge box on the left hanging from a shoulder belt. A waist belt held the sword or saber, and pistol holsters were fixed to the front of the saddle. The particular arms and equipment of the Cuera cavalrymen were as described above and in the captions to the color plates and illustrations.

SELECT BIBLIOGRAPHY

Most of the data in this book is taken from manuscript documents held in archives and libraries in Spain, Mexico and the United States; for these sources, see the Author's Note on the imprint page at the beginning of this book. Some of the more useful printed sources are listed below:

Abelardo, Carrillo y Gabriel, *El Traje en la Nueva Espana* (Mexico, 1959)

Albi, Julio, *La Defensa de Indias 1764–1799* (ICI, Madrid, 1987)

Bancroft, Hubert Howe, *History of North Mexican States and Texas* (San Francisco, 1884); *California Pastoral* (1888); and *History of Arizona and New Mexico* (1889)

Brinckerhoff, Sydney B., & Pierce A. Chamberlain, *Spanish Military Weapons in Colonial America 1700–1821* (Harrisburg, PA, 1972)

Brinckerhoff, Sydney B., & Odie B. Faulk, *Lancers for the King* (Pheonix, AZ, 1965)

Bueno, José M., *Tropas Virreynales: (1) Nueva Espana, Yucatan y Luisiana* (Malaga, 1983)

Calvo, Juan L., *Armamento reglamento y auxiliar del ejercito español*, Vol.1 (Barcelona, 1975)

Carmen Velasquez, *Maria del, El Estado de Guerra en Nueva España 1760–1808* (Mexico, 1950)

Codonach, Guadalupe Jiménez, *Mexico su tiempo de nacer 1750–1821* (Banamex, Mexico, 1997)

Colomar Albajar, Maria Antonia, *Archivo General de India: Catalogo de Uniformes, seccion de mapas y planos* (Madrid, 1981)

Clonard, Conde de, *Historia organica de las armas de infanteria y caballeria españolas*, Vols. 5 to 16 (Madrid, 1851–1859)

Estado Mayor Central del Ejercito, *Heraldica e Historiales del Ejercito*, Vols. 3 to 10 (Madrid, 1973–1993)

Estado Militar de Espana (Madrid) for 1769, 1777, 1795 & 1800, and *…de Nueva Espana* (Mexico) for 1787 & 1788

Fernandez, Juan Marchena, *Officiales y soldados en el ejercito de America* (Seville, 1983)

Finke, Detmar, "La organizacion del ejercito en Nueva Espana," in *Boletin del Archivo General de la Nacion*, XI: 4 (September- December 1940)

Haarmann, Albert W., "The Siege of Pensacola: an Order of Battle," in *Florida Historical Quarterly*, 44: 3 (January 1966)

Holmes, Jack D.L., *Honor and Fidelity: The Louisiana Infantry Regiment and the Louisiana Militia Companies 1766–1821* (Birmingham, AL, 1965)

Naylor, Thomas H., & Charles W. Polzer, *Pedro de Rivera and the Military Regulation for Northern New Spain 1724–1729* (Tucson, AZ, 1986)

McAllister, Lyle, *The "Fuero Militar" in New Spain 1764–1800* (University of Florida, Gainesville, 1957)

Moorhead, Max L., Th*e Presidio: Bastion of the Spanish Borderlands* (Norman, OK, 1975)

Moreno, Justa, " 'Teatro Militar de Europa', Manuscrito de la Biblioteca de Palacio," in *Reales Sitios*, XI, No. 42 (Cuatro Trimester 1974)

Ordenanzas de S.M. para el regimen, disciplina, subordinacion, y servicio de sus exercitos... (Madrid, 1768)

Ramirez, Bibiano Torres, *La Isla de Puerto Rico 1765–1800* (San Juan, 1968)

Ruiz Gomez, M., & V. Alonso Juanola, *El Ejercito de los Borbones*, Vols I to III (Madrid, 1989–1992)

Sanchez, Joseph P., *Spanish Bluecoats: The Catalonian Volunteers in Northwestern New Spain 1767–1810* (Albuquerque, NM, 1990)

Tepaske, John Jay, *The Government of Spanish Florida 1700–1763* (Duke University, Durham, 1964)

Vigon, Jorge, *Historia de la Artilleria Espanola*, Vols 1 & 2 (Madrid, 1947)

PLATE COMMENTARIES

A: FLORIDA & WEST INDIES, c.1730s–1763

A1: Infantry private, 1735–40

From the various cloth shipments sent to Florida and Havana, the most likely resulting uniform would be a blue coat (possibly unlined) with red cuffs, a red waistcoat, brass buttons, blue breeches, red stockings, a black tricorn hat edged with yellow or false gold lace and bearing a red cockade, a linen shirt and cravat, and shoes. Note the large "belly box" for musket cartridges, and the separate powder flask. (Documentary sources: UFSC, AGI 58-2-4 and 58-1-34/64)

A2: Infantry officer, c.1740

The officers' uniforms for all regular colonial infantry units stationed in Florida and the West Indies were generally similar to those of their men, but better tailored from materials of superior quality. They usually wore blue faced with scarlet, with gold buttons and gold hat lace. No lace was allowed on the coat, and there were no uniform rank distinctions until 1768 – though note the regulation cane. They were armed with swords and, for formal occasions, spontoons. (ASKB, 1740s Ms)

A3: Artillery gunner, c.1755

In April 1753 the four artillery companies of the Havana Regiment were ordered to wear a "red cloth coat and breeches, with blue cuffs, waistcoat and blue stockings, and with the corresponding lace and sword knot, giving the sergeants and corporals the rank distinctions on their clothing the same as that which is provided for the regiment in Article 42, and the accoutrements to be the same." (AGN, Bandos, Vol. 4)

The hair was officially worn powdered until 1791; and Spanish soldiers were almost invariably clean-shaven during the 18th century.

B: THE NORTHERN INTERIOR PROVINCES

B1: Trooper, Cuera cavalry, mid-18th century

According to the account of the engineer Miguel Costanza in 1791, the leather jacket or *cuera* reached down to the knees, having "the shape of a coat without sleeves... made of seven plies of white tanned deerskin, which protects against the arrows of the Indians except at a very short range." Although supposed to be bleached white, the outer hides were sometimes of other hues. In March 1767 the Marquis de Rubi found the leather jackets dyed yellow at Buenavista, and of a cinnamon color at Coahuila. Artwork of the period usually shows the *cuera* as a long sleeveless garment that often appears to bear decorative work; for example, in Sonora, seams and pockets decorated with a lining of filigreed leather and red cloth were popular. At San Francisco, California, the trooper José Maria Amador recalled that the leather jacket was made in three sections "like a vest," held together with buckskin straps under the arms, and coming "down to about the knee...."

A shorter version of the *cuera* evolved in Texas during the late 18th century, but apparently not in California. The soldiers' clothing during the second third of the 18th century was generally blue and red, although details certainly varied greatly. During inspection in Texas, Rubi found the soldiers at San Antonio wearing pretty much what they pleased, predominantly in "various shades of red... [with] white silk handkerchiefs and lace, and silver buttons." When he got to Loreto the garrison was in its "best uniforms," consisting of red jackets and red breeches adorned with metal buttons. He concluded that the uniform must be simplified, with red facings confined to the collar of the blue coat. (Father Tirsch drawings made in Lower California c.1767, in the State Library, Prague; AGI, Guadalajara

Gunner, Puerto Rico regular artillery, 1785; watercolor by José Campeche. This company was part of the overseas establishment of the Royal Corps of Artillery, and besides a hundred gunners it also included a 14-man squad of miners. Its regular uniform was the corps' conventional blue and red – see Plate A3. However, like other units in tropical stations, it also had a light cloth and linen uniform; this consisted of a white coat, waistcoat and breeches, with blue collar, cuffs, and buttonhole lace at the front, gold buttons, and gold lace edging to the collar and hat. Buff accoutrements included a slot on the crossbelt for the vent prickers, and a black ventral cartridge box stamped with the royal arms on its flap. This was a garrison unit, mostly serving the heavy guns in the extensive San Juan fortifications, so no marching gaiters are shown. (Uniforme 115; Archivo General de Indias, Sevilla)

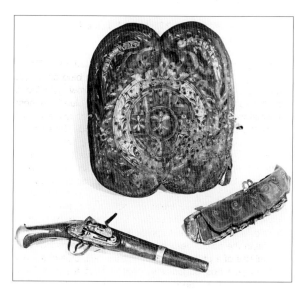

A "Cuera" cavalryman's leather shield, painted with a crude version of the Spanish coat of arms; a much-repaired pistol with a miquelet lock; and a wide ventral cartridge box – see Plate B. The *adarga* shield is an intriguing survival; originally a North African form, it can be traced to the wars of the Spanish *Reconquista* as early as the 14th century. (Collection and photo Los Angeles County Museum of Natural History, Los Angeles)

271, 283; BLCA, Ms D-28; Rubi quoted in Carlos L. Castaneda, *Our Catholic Heritage in Texas*, Austin, 1939)

B2: Trooper, Cuera cavalry, as 1772 regulations
One of the most important documents on the Cuera cavalry and the network of presidios is the regulation of 10 September 1772. This was the first document signed by royal authority to specify in detail the uniform, arms and equipment for these troops. Each soldier had "a short, sleeved waistcoat of blue wool velvet or cloth, with small scarlet cuffs and collar; breeches of blue wool velvet; cape of wool of the same color; cartridge box, *cuera* and bandoleer of sueded leather, of the sort that is currently in use, and embroidered on the bandoleer [with] the name of the presidio, by which to distinguish each [presidial company] from the others; black neck stock, hat, shoes and leggings." The buttons were of yellow metal. (AGI, Guadalajara 522).

B3: Trooper, Cuera cavalry, undress uniform, c.1780s
Undress and fatigue uniforms were sometimes worn according to local initiatives. During an expedition against the Indians in Texas during 1787, troopers wore "jackets and breeches of tanned leather and blankets which were an inconspicuous shade of brown, the best color to prevent their being seen from afar." Instructions given at Santa Barbara on 16 June 1797 for California troops undoubtedly formalized long-existing practices. They specified that "for the different types of work which the troops do... they may use breeches and short jacket of dyed leather with scarlet cloth or 'tripe' [a wool velvet material] collar and cuffs, gold buttons, keeping the scarlet waistcoat for holidays and for mounting guard at the Presidio... when they must wear the full uniform." (Juan de Ugalde, "Diary...January to August 1787," *Texas Military History*, II: 4, November 1962; BLCA 7, MP257).

C: CALIFORNIA & NORTHWEST COAST, 1769–1790s

C1: Officer, Cuera cavalry, undress, 1780
According to the 21 September 1780 regulations, officers were to have a dress uniform consisting of a blue coat with scarlet collar, cuffs and lapels, with two narrow gold laces each "three threads" wide edging the collar; blue breeches; buff waistcoat, with gold lace "slightly wider than two fingers," gold buttons, and a tricorn hat laced with gold. The officers' undress uniform was a short blue coat with the same facings as on the dress coat; a short linen, chamois or buff cloth waistcoat edged with a narrow lace; cloth or chamois breeches; a black hat with the brim turned up on one side and laced with gold; and a cape of blue cloth. Gold epaulettes according to rank were worn on both the dress and the undress coats. The undress uniform was always to be worn in the field, and during the summer it could be made of light material in the colors described above. Other items included optional use of a protective *redecilla* (hair net), blue or scarlet (as here) ponchos edged with gold lace at the openings, chamois leggings, and Mexican-style "vaquero" horse equipment. The arms of the officers were the same as those of the troops, but of better quality – in this case an *escopeta* carbine as well as a sword. Officers also had the leather jacket and shield. (BLCA 15, IV).

C2: Trooper, Ligera cavalry, c.1778–83
The first Commandant-General of the Interior Provinces, Teodoro de Croix, did not think much of the leather jacket, judging it too bulky and impairing rapid movement. This was one reason for his creation of the Tropas Ligeras (light troops) companies in 1778. These light cavalry had the same uniform,

Lieutenant Jean-Baptiste MacCarty, New Orleans Distinguished Carabinier Cavalry Company, c.1785–93, in a portrait attributed to J. Salazar. This militia company was raised in 1779 amongst the New Orleans gentry and artisans. The uniform was a "puce" (shown as a rich crimson) coat with white collar, lapels, cuffs and turnbacks, a white waistcoat and breeches, with gold buttons and buttonhole lace, and gold epaulets for officers. MacCarty was commissioned sub-lieutenant in August 1779, lieutenant in July 1780, and captain in November 1793; here he wears the lieutenant's single gold-strapped epaulet on the right shoulder. Compare with Plate D2. (Louisiana State Museum, New Orleans)

equipment and weapons as the Cuera companies, but without the leather jacket, shield or lance. According to the 1780 orders upon which we base our figure, they were to have a white hat instead of a black one. However, only a year later Governor Cabello of Texas believed that ten Cuera soldiers were worth twenty of the light horsemen. His colleague, Governor Ugalde of Coahuila, felt much the same, also having a preference for cinnamon-colored leather jackets in 1782. After de Croix's departure in 1783 the light troops gradually vanished from the order of battle. (AGI, Guadalajara 272, 283)

C3: Private, Catalonian Volunteer companies, c.1767–94
Each private had a black tricorn edged with white lace and bearing the red cockade. The *gambeta* style of coat, made of wool cloth, was of ample cut, and its lining was not turned back as on ordinary Army-style coats. It was blue with a yellow collar and cuffs, blue cuff flaps and white metal buttons, and was lined with a light wool material. The yellow waistcoat illustrated here had a blue collar and cuffs and small white metal buttons. The shirt was white and the cravat black; breeches were blue, the stockings white, and there was also a fatigue cap, probably with a blue bag above a yellow turn-up. Corporals had the same uniform but with double silver lace edging the collar, or single lace for second corporals. Sergeants did not have *gambetas*, but wore the standard Army-style coat of blue cloth with yellow collar and cuffs, blue cuff flaps, blue turnbacks and silver buttons. Their insignia of rank were epaulets of silver lace mixed with yellow silk, worn on both shoulders of the coat, and they also had mixed silver and yellow silk sword knots. The rest of their uniform was the same as for the enlisted men. It has been stated that they carried *escopeta* light muskets, but both the regiment in Old Spain and the companies in New Spain carried the standard M1757 military musket with its bayonet. Initially, the company sent to New Spain was armed with pistols as was traditional for Catalonian mountain troops, but only a few survived the Sonora expedition, and none were issued when the companies were re-armed in 1773 and in 1790. The corporals and drummers also had a hanger, and sergeants a sword. (AGN, Guerra Indeferente 146, 168 and Historia 213)

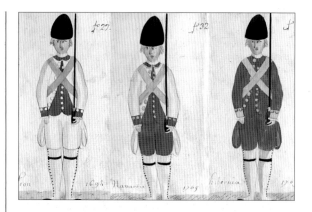

Grenadiers of the metropolitan Leon, Navarra and Hibernia infantry regiments, from a manuscript of 1780. All three units were present at the capture of Pensacola from the British in 1781, and all have black bearskin caps, white gaiters and buff accoutrements:
Leon – white coat and breeches, scarlet collar, cuffs and waistcoat, silver buttons; Navarra – white coat, scarlet collar edged with gold lace, scarlet cuffs, waistcoat and breeches, gold buttons; Hibernia (see Plate F2) – collarless red coat, waistcoat and breeches, green cuffs, silver buttons. (Anne S.K. Brown Military Collection, Brown University Library, Providence, USA)

D: COLONIAL TROOPS, LOUISIANA, 1769–1780s

D1: Private, Luisiana Regiment, c.1780
The regiment's uniform adopted in 1770 was a white coat with blue collar, cuffs, turnbacks, waistcoat and breeches, with white metal buttons and white hat lace. (AGI, Cuba 2360)

D2: Officer, St Louis militia cavalry, 1779
This mounted unit raised early in 1779 was obviously made up of wealthy young gentlemen. That July it was reported by the commandant of St Louis as wearing "coat and breeches red, cuffs, waistcoat and lapels blue, buttons gilt." Governor Galvez was pleased to learn of the formation of this unit, and approved its uniform in August 1779.

D3: Officer, New Orleans militia battalion, c.1780
Organized in 1770, the five city companies were formed into a battalion that included a grenadier company in 1775. The uniform, probably limited largely to the officers, was a blue coat and breeches with scarlet collar, cuffs, lapels and waistcoat, with gold buttons and hat lace. (AGI, Cuba 2360; copy in Library of Congress of the Carta de Galvez at the Cuban archives)

E: COLONIAL TROOPS, LOUISIANA & FLORIDA, 1770–1780s

E1: Grenadier, Havana Regiment, 1769–86
From 1769 the regiment's uniform consisted of a blue coat and breeches, with yellow collar, cuffs and waistcoat and yellow metal buttons. The color of the linings (and therefore the turnbacks) appears to have been blue until 1788. The fusiliers' hat was laced with "false gold" (a mixture of yellow silk thread and copper); grenadiers and sappers had fur caps with a long yellow bag embroidered with false gold. From the mid-1780s, Spanish Army bearskin caps had a small yellow metal grenade badge on the front, and this is mentioned for the Havana Regiment from 1787. (AGI, Santo Domingo 2163)

E2: Drummer, Luisiana Regiment, 1770s–80s
From March 1760, drummers and fifers in the Spanish forces were required to wear the colors of the royal livery: blue coat and breeches, scarlet collar, cuffs and waistcoat, the coat and waistcoat trimmed with the king's livery lace, and regimental buttons and hat lace – which, for the Luisiana Regiment, were white metal and white lace. Drums were generally painted in the coat color, with the royal arms painted on the side. (AGS, Guerra Moderna 2986)

E3: Private, Luisiana Dragoon company, 1780s
This company was raised in 1780 with picked men from the Mexico and Nueva Espana dragoon regiments, and took part in the 1781 Pensacola campaign. Besides its purely military duties it also served as a gendarmerie, based in New Orleans to ensure that soldiers and civilians did not become overly rowdy; the dragoons patrolled highways, and looked out for runaway slaves. The company's uniform was a blue coat with scarlet collar, cuffs, lapels and waistcoat, blue breeches, yellow metal buttons and hat lace. (AGI, Cuba 2360)

F: METROPOLITAN TROOPS, LOUISIANA & FLORIDA, 1770s–80s

F1: First Sergeant of a fusilier company, Toledo Regiment
The Toledo Regiment's uniform was a white coat with blue collar, cuffs, waistcoat and breeches, gold buttons and hat lace. It was one of the few regiments that had a three-point cuff flap of the coat color. Sergeants were distinguished by fringed epaulets of the facing color, first sergeants having one on each shoulder. All NCOs were armed with musket, bayonet and hanger. (ASKB 1777 and 1780 Mss)

F2: Private of a fusilier company, Hibernia Regiment
Like the other Irish regiments in Spanish service, Hibernia had a scarlet uniform with gold buttons and lace. It was distinguished by its green cuffs, and its coat had no collar. (ASKB 1777 and 1780 Mss)

F3: Grenadier, Rey Regiment
Until 1766 this was the Grenada Regiment, retitled the Rey (King's) that year; its previously white uniform with violet facings was changed to blue in 1773. It was nicknamed "Immemorial del Rey" because of its ancient origins. At the time of the American War of Independence it wore a blue coat and breeches with a scarlet collar, cuffs and waistcoat, gold buttons and buttonhole lace on the coat and waistcoat. The buttonhole lace is shown on both sides of the coat front in the 1777 manuscript and the 1785 chart, but the 1780 manuscript shows the buttonholes laced only on the coat's left side. The grenadiers wore the bearskin cap with a long, pointed bag in scarlet, decorated with gold lace and bearing the embroidered royal arms. (ASKB 1777 and 1780 Mss; Clonard, *Historia organica…*VIII)

G: LOUISIANA, FLORIDA & CENTRAL AMERICA, 1770s–80s

G1: Private, Espana Regiment
From 24 October 1776, Spanish soldiers were also authorized an undress uniform consisting of a white jacket with collar and cuffs of the facing color, regimental buttons, and "a small cap," which appears to have been of the coat color with the turn-up and piping of facing color. According to an order of 17 April 1768, the cap may also have been black with a vizor that could be turned up, but clothing bills usually mention a cloth cap of the uniform's basic and facing colors. Espana's undress jacket

would have had green collar and cuffs and gold buttons; the cap has a green turn-up, and green piping and tassel decorating its white pointed bag.

G2: Private of a fusilier company, Principe Regiment, c.1775–82

For the warm season overseas, troops leaving Spain to serve in America were issued a white linen uniform. The coat probably had the collar, cuffs and buttons of the regimental colors, as was the case for colonial units in tropical stations. For Principe, this would mean a scarlet collar and cuffs and silver buttons. When it was sent to Cuba in 1771 the regiment's uniform was a blue coat and breeches, scarlet collar, cuffs and waistcoat, with silver buttons and buttonhole lace. The blue was changed to white in the mid-1770s; back in Spain from 1782, Principe's regular uniform had changed back to blue and scarlet by 1784–85. (ASKB 1777 and 1780 Mss; Clonard, *Historia organica…VIII*)

G3: Captain, Fijo de Guatemala Regiment

This regiment, raised in 1777, was involved in the still relatively unknown campaigns against the British in Honduras. It had a white linen uniform with blue collar and cuffs and yellow buttons, the collar having a yellow laced edge and the cuffs having three buttons. For officers the buttons were gold, and the collars and hats were edged with gold lace. Company officers wore gold epaulets (one on both shoulders for captains), and gilt gorgets when on duty; they carried muskets, with pouch and sword/bayonet belts of the facing color, edged with lace of the button color. (Gomez and Juanola, *El Ejercito de los Borbones*, tome III: vol. I)

H: DRAGOONS, ENGINEERS & ARTILLERY, 1770s–80s

H1: Private, Guatemala Dragoons, c.1779–82

This "disciplined militia" unit – which had four squadrons, each of three companies – appears to have been partly or completely mobilized in 1779–83, and acted as quasi-regular dragoons in the campaigns against the British, seemingly serving mostly on foot. The uniform for the Guatemala disciplined militia mounted units was blue with scarlet cuffs, yellow metal buttons, and dragoon-style gaiters. The Guatemala Dragoons were said to have a "cap with plumes," which would have been similar to those worn by dragoons in Spain – of black leather, edged with black plumes, with a brass front plate or badge and a red feather on the left side. (Gomez and Juanola, *El Ejercito de los Borbones*, tome III: vol. I)

H2: Officer, Royal Corps of Engineers, c.1770

A service dress for the engineers was authorized in February 1762, and an order of 22 October 1768 prescribed it in detail – a blue coat and breeches, with scarlet collar, cuffs and waistcoat, silver buttons and lace. There was silver lace edging to the coat fronts, collar, cuffs, and pocket flaps and decorating the buttonholes, and the waistcoat was similarly laced. A 1789 watercolor shows a very plain uniform, with broad silver lace edging the collar and cuffs only. (AGS, Guerra Moderna 2986; ASKB 1789 Ms)

H3: Gunner, Royal Corps of Artillery

From the early 18th century the metropolitan artillery wore a blue uniform with scarlet cuffs and waistcoat, and gold buttons and hat lace. A scarlet collar was added by the 1760s, and in 1771 a yellow lace edging was added to the collar (sergeants had double-width lace). The forage cap was edged with a "gold colored" lace, stockings were white, and a linen waistcoat and breeches were also issued for warm weather. From the 1760s, this uniform was officially the same

for all artillery units in Spain and throughout its empire. In November 1773 a ten-year renewable contract specified buff accoutrement belts; note the brass pouch flap badges and pricker case. Between 1773 and 1784 enlisted gunners did not have short swords. Officers had gold lace edging to their coats and waistcoats. (AGS, Tesoro, Inv. 25, Leg. 17; Carlos Medina Avila, *Organizacion y uniformes de la artilleria Espanola*, Madrid, 1992)

Colonel Ignacio Mascaro y Homar, Royal Corps of Engineers, c.1790s. From the 1780s he was the chief engineer at San Juan, Puerto Rico, and in 1797 the British found his improved fortifications effectively impregnable. He is shown in the engineers' full dress uniform, which featured wide silver lace edging to the coat's front, collar, pockets and cuffs, with three narrow silver laces on each cuff indicating his rank of colonel; compare this with Plate H2, illustrating a plainer service uniform of 20 years previously. This portrait has been wrongly identified as Governor de Ustariz. (Print after José Campeche; private collection)

INDEX